Keeping Afloat

Also from Loose Chippings Books

The Cheesemonger's Tales
A good read for all food and wine lovers

Not Dark Yet
A very funny book about cricket

Cool Is The Reaping
Poems of rural England

Diary of a Shropshire Lass
A delightful autobiography

The Harts of Chipping Campden
Essential reading for all who admire the town or fine silver

Full details from our website
www.loosechippings.org

Keeping Afloat

Up a French canal
.....without a paddle

John Liley

First Published 2009

Cover Illustration: Diane Fine

Published by
Loose Chippings Books
The Paddocks
Chipping Campden
Gloucestershire
GL55 6AU
www.loosechippings.org

Typeset in Baskerville

Printed in England by J F Print Limited, Sparkford

ISBN 978-0-9554217-5-4

Dedication

To all who thought it should be fun

CONTENTS

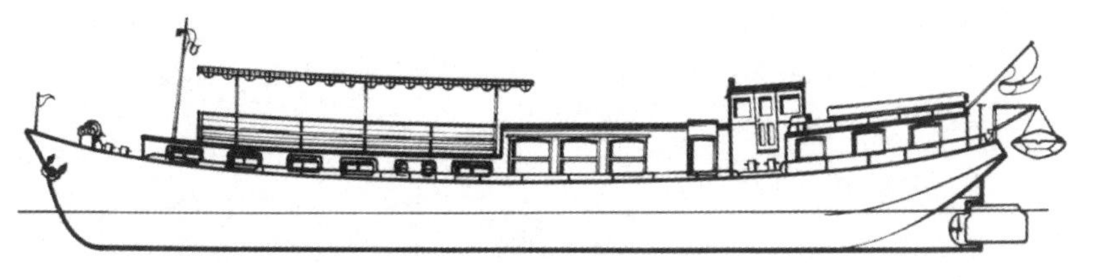

Secunda

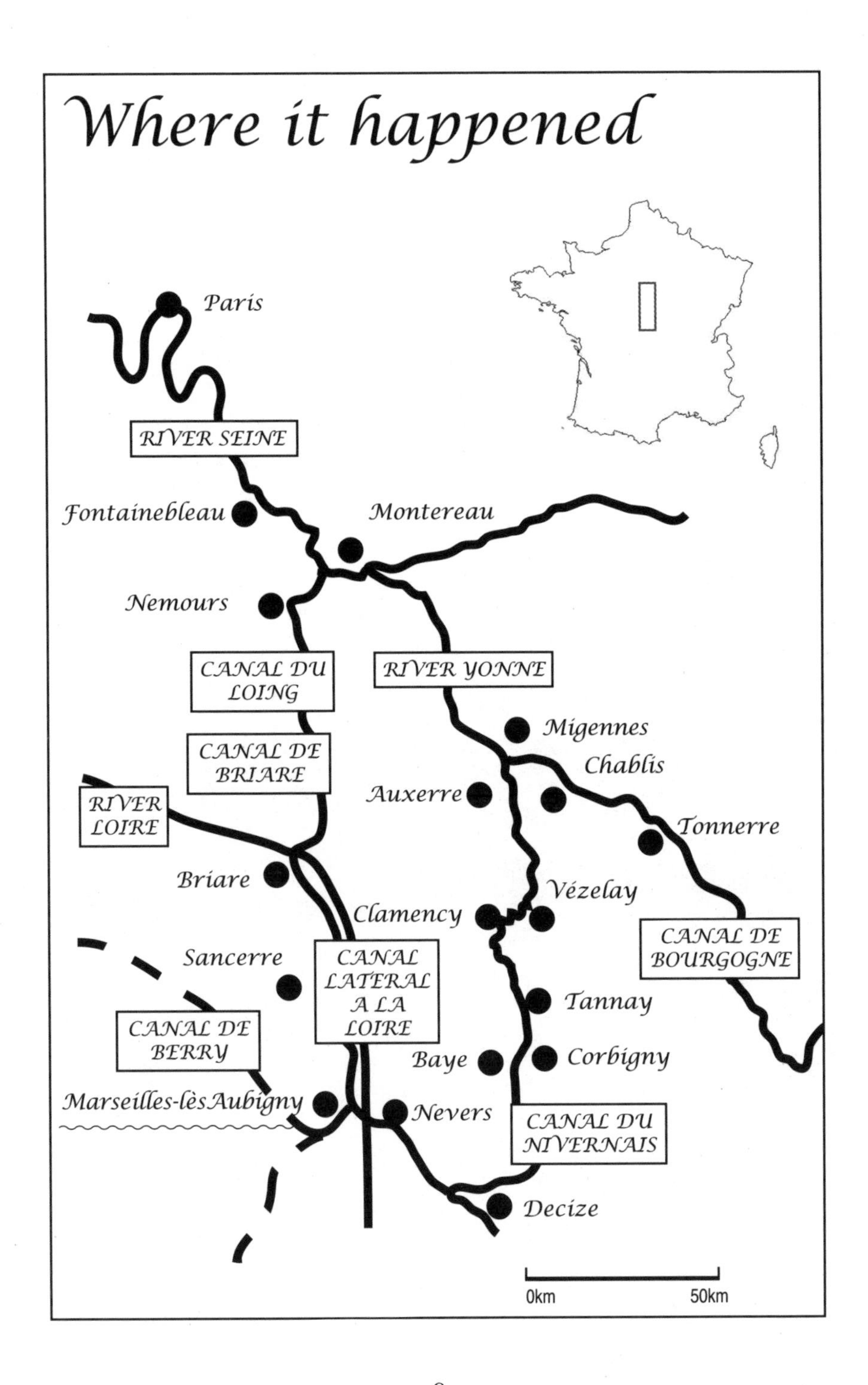
Where it happened
Paris
RIVER SEINE
Fontainebleau
Montereau
Nemours
CANAL DU LOING
RIVER YONNE
Migennes
Chablis
CANAL DE BRIARE
Auxerre
RIVER LOIRE
Tonnerre
Briare
Vézelay
Clamency
CANAL DE BOURGOGNE
Sancerre
CANAL LATERAL A LA LOIRE
Tannay
CANAL DE BERRY
Baye
Corbigny
Marseilles-lès Aubigny
Nevers
CANAL DU NIVERNAIS
Decize
0km
50km

THE SITUATION

Voices carry over water. Surprising things may be overheard, even on a canal. 'He's a funny bugger isn't he?' came to me once, with the ego-puncturing follow-up: 'Laughs at his own jokes and doesn't listen to a single ..... word you say.' At Marseilles-lès-Aubigny, many years ago, it happened yet again.

We had set up in business, the group of us, with a passenger-carrying barge on Burgundy's western edge. And, straight away, we were struggling. The money had gone, mine certainly had, and customers were few. In a strange land, a good deal stranger than we'd imagined it to be, those were bothersome times.

The country beside the canal there, of farmland often, provides glimpses of the sprawling upper Loire. It is agreeable if largely unremarkable, with Marseilles-lès-Aubigny itself, within sight of a cement works, one of the lesser spots. On the way, though, there are finer sights: vineyards on the hillsides of Sancerre, poplars shading the old towing path, eagles over the cornfields. It helps, if following this route, not to be in a hurry.

A motor boat was passing, a rakish thing, with assertive-looking people on board and seriously slanted windows. She was, without doubt, making for the Mediterranean, taking her chance amongst the freight barges and bashing about in the locks. Her crew, if they were typical, would be finding the canal system tiresome.

'We might as well stop,' came a voice. 'We can moor against that old black barge over there. Ask that cretin in the wheelhouse if he can help.'

'*Monsieur*,' his wife began to call. '*Monsieur, est-ce que voo …*'

'*Non*,' I was able to reply.

'Oh, we'll press on,' the first voice continued. 'Leave him alone. He wouldn't be able to help, you can tell. Looks a real canal-type idiot. Anyone with a barge like that must be a nutcase anyway.'

'It takes one to know one.' I might have responded, but for some reason found myself trying to compose that in French. As to the nutcase part, I was beginning to wonder if he was right.

1: SETTING OUT

The business with the barge developed out of desperation. The others involved, being richer, or at least in salaried employment, had been intrigued enough to join for the ride. So we formed a company to move the project on. It was launched formally, if that's the word, one foggy autumn evening in an office off Oxford Street in London.

Our initial meeting was interrupted, in a tradition that would develop, by the arrival of the cleaning woman. As an example of the surprises lying ahead this was by no means a big one; but we were startled all the same. As if in a pantomime, the door shot open, a sack of rubbish arrived, then in she came. Headscarf rampant, vacuum cleaner at the ready, she was complaining about the lights and the need to turn them off when we went. If we did not, Mister someone we had never met would be having our guts for garters.

The intruder retreated as the accountant, who was presiding, put on a withering look and willed her out of the door. The office had been rented for the evening but, knowing more than we did, if not the cleaning woman's boss, our man kept his coat on throughout. There was trouble with the heating apparently and it got no better as the hours went by.

There were eight in our company. Some were old pals; some I'd bumped into, friends of friends or contacts through work. One of us - Hector - had been found through advertising. It was a ridiculous number, of course, as those who claimed to really know about business were touchingly keen to advise. Disharmony was bound to follow, they said. Never go into such things with your pals. And so on.

It was not a new idea. Others had tried it before, although not many, and all of those - or almost all - had been doing so in England. Few, very few indeed, ever ran a barge in France. I had, in fact, met the first of them a decade or so earlier, way back in 1964, when he came to see us at the office of a boating magazine I worked for in London. Richard Parsons was his name, and he was trying to get publicity.

He came along on the day we went to press, always a tricky time, when, with the oaths of our printers echoing down the telephone, we struggled to caption such pictures as we managed to find and get all the copy to fit. 'There's some bastard in Reception,' somebody said. As the new boy in our office, I was the one sent to meet him.

Richard's hair, a fraction too long for the day, spoke of priorities elsewhere. Tall and amiable, he had a faintly abstracted air. His overcoat, presumably bought in France, was unusually cut, and a little too long as well. He came from Wolverhampton, he said, yet was no longer Wolverhampton. It was a manner designed for survival, I would discover; the protective shell of someone who, confronted by worries he never expected, in a land where many things are different, was aiming somehow to carry on.

Under the eye of the company commissionaire, sitting in the lobby like the recruiting poster from the First World War, we looked at Richard's photos together. Small and curly ones these were. What they were of was difficult at first to make out. The Eiffel Tower offered up a clue. So the waterway must have been the Seine, while the vessel in the foreground, like a sausage with a shed on top, was presumably …

'… the barge,' Richard said. 'We're fitting her out.' He rolled his eyes as he said this. Barge conversion, as I would discover myself one day, is a conjuror's box of puzzlements, of problems unforeseen and solutions born of desperation. That it is hideously expensive as well takes even the experienced by surprise.

A wash-basin winked from one of the pictures, against a background of pipes yet to be boarded in. There was a saloon, with windows from a retired city bus, while the labour force, apparently friends from England, stood around with looks of pride in their work.

This alone was a surprise. For Brits to be working in France was not such a commonplace then. To someone as wary of foreign parts as myself they seemed extremely brave. France at the time was a far-off land. It had a different kind of culture, with a language few in Britain ever troubled to learn. The French, it was popularly understood, were haughty and uncooperative. They closed their shops at lunchtime and undercooked their meat. Those who visited the country did so, generally, in a spirit of apprehension, then seemed glad to get back.

Richard had christened his barge *Palinurus* - someone in Greek mythology, whose background he explained, but I immediately forgot. Prior to this, as a coal boat near Dunkerque, the name had been *Ponctuel*, a commitment too dangerous to continue, even for the starry-eyed.

Burgundy was the region the *Palinurus* would be exploring, the dukedom of the Vagabond King and the home of quality wine, although it was unusual in Britain to drink it and the general concept was vague. Burgundy, indeed, like so much else in France, was a grey area of the English mind, to be filed with Transylvania or Lilliput. It was a surprise to learn it really existed, but Richard said it was beautiful. There were waterways there apparently: both rivers and canals, and those were beautiful too.

'Can you help?' Richard asked again, and I said we would try. We shook hands and he left.

To our eternal discredit, we did nothing much about it. An item appeared buried in some text about 'developments', while the pictures, as they do with magazines, lingered in a drawer for a while; then they disappeared.

Eventually, I was to explore those waterways myself, even meeting Richard again once or twice. There he was, several years later on, guiding *Palinurus* along the canal south of Auxerre. With a full load of passengers, in surroundings gorgeous enough for a calendar, he managed, nonetheless, to look abstracted again. The cook had handed in her notice, we discovered, while he was under the threat of a tax control. Even the strong and upright quail before a tax control in France, which takes on the aura of 'When did you last see your father'. The force with which Richard described these matters drew some attention to their importance; although little did I realise how really mind-blowing such crises might be.

Encountered again a few weeks later near Dijon, he was in a mellower mood. The tax inspection had somehow been diverted, while a cook miraculously turned up, just as the crew were wringing their hands. There were business partners, apparently, who managed these things (and who also, in the years to come, would expand the operation by acquiring other barges). That he had such colleagues would never have occurred to me, nor the incidents they had to resolve. It would be years before the memory of these events returned - when the same things happened to me.

Those early trips that my friends and I were making were for our own amusement - in an English barge named *Arthur*. In the *Arthur*, having thrown up the job with the magazine, I could travel around for two long summers, with a spell back in London in between, earning the money to pay for it all. In those halcyon days, when other jobs could always be found - or so it seemed - it was easy to take such chances.

Out on the *Arthur* the fear of France - or rather of the French - had by no means disappeared. Those invited out to join us were often in awe of the place too. At the rendezvous we arranged, usually at the railway station on a Saturday afternoon, they would be sitting with their rucksacks, like pioneers with the wagons drawn round, staring at the natives. The differences between first and second-class train compartments often confounded them. A child of ten could have detected the reason why one set of carriages should be packed while another part stood empty but, frequently, there had been arguments about this. Occasionally, even, there was a fine, when the conductor came down the train doing Bonaparte imitations. There were problems of pronunciation too, requests for tickets to Nangcy or Tchallon-sewer-Sone proving not to be understood.

In the evenings, when we weren't cooking up spaghetti Bolognese, we would march down the towpath to whatever *estaminet* the village might provide. There, tongues loosened by alcohol, the party, in dreadful French, would order snails, complemented by more-ish, crusty bread in order to mop up the sauce, before tucking into the *plat du jour*. Even at the budget end of the spectrum, the meals, by and large, exceeded by a mile what might have been found in England. Funnily enough, it is the marginal suppers that stick in the mind, the ones on the level of the proverbial Greasy Spoon.

'Is Horse the only thing you've got?' we asked at an *auberge* in Alsace.

'It's the speciality of the house, sir,' came the quick-witted reply. And so, washed down with corrosive *vin ordinaire*, another little adventure ran its course.

At Montereau on the Seine, in the only place we could find there, the noise from the table football or *babyfoot*, (pronounced babby-foot) combined with the din from those locals not playing *babyfoot* themselves, supplemented by *Taras Bulba* on TV, brought the conversational level to the threshold of pain. When the ball bounced free for a moment, to splash in one of our party's stew, there was something about the situation to lift a meal that, by French standards, was scarcely mediocre, to a positive social event. We played the locals at *babyfoot* later, losing ten-nil and nine-one (a lucky rebound there) then settled on a further round of drinks.

A major regret, now, was our lack of interest in the wine. Conditioned by the soft, blended rubbish we had been in the habit of drinking in England, we were in no fit state for the splendours of France. Hypnotised by extremely agreeable prices, we would buy, even so, the cheapest that they had. On this, if we were prepared to carry back the empties, we even got refunds on the bottles.

But the countryside reached us. It was splendid, and there was a great deal of it. An elderly guy with a handlebar moustache stopped by the roadside one morning in his old Citroën, somewhere to the west of Auxonne, to give a pair of us a lift towards the river. He looked at first like a character out of a Tin-Tin book, a benign uncle-like figure from an era half-forgotten; but he was real enough. He had a hamper with him, from which he offered cheese and a dash of something alcoholic as we headed for the Saône. There, in a spot that he knew, he would be settling down to fish. With cattle browsing in the shallows of the opposite bank, he could loll in the Arcadian splendour that the river's upper reaches so generously provide. Kenneth Graham summoned up a similar vision of England, where, despite the pressures of population, it still exists in pockets. But in France it is all around.

After the glories of rural France, returning to London to a proper job was difficult indeed. But a new magazine was starting up and it had its attractions. Chief amongst these, of course, was the salary. On the down side were the crowds to jostle with, all those people in suits.

On the very first morning a humbling incident took place. As the tube train rolled to a stop, its carriages so packed that if anyone wanted to read a book, let alone a newspaper, they might only have done so by raising it towards the ceiling, a middle-aged woman, extracting herself through the doorway, turned to address us from the platform.

'Is this,' she said, 'how you go to work each day? Packed in here like cattle? Then…' The finale, so obvious it was boring to have to wait for it, hove into view at last: '… I feel darned sorry for you all.'

That old man beside the Saône, scattering his ground-bait, would undoubtedly have agreed. But in London, of course, no-one said anything at all. It was all too depressing.

There was no great need to have worried. With the outbreak of war in the Middle East, an economic whirlwind arrived. The government was under threat. There were power cuts and, by Parliamentary edict, a three-day working week. The magazine collapsed without a single issue printed.

The possibilities, suddenly, were bleak. Inflation was soaring. Those of us who were leaving - paid off well, it has to be said - had to decide very quickly what to do with our savings.

In a shabby basement flat in west London - rented, rather than owned - there was time now to listen on the radio to the steady succession of folk who, despite the good fortune of remaining in employment, were angling for increases in their pay. Doctors lobbied for, and got, a salary rise of 38%. In a climate such as this savings shrink very quickly. Something would have to be done. But what, exactly? What?

Vaguely, the notion developed of going through the *Arthur* experience once again, though that boat had now been sold. It would need a bigger barge anyway, if a living was to be made at it.

A bigger barge … And here, through information only a canal enthusiast might obtain, lay a possible chance. In the Netherlands, under a government scheme, barges were being sold at rock-bottom prices. If ever the *Arthur* idea could be repeated, on the scale that was necessary, now might be the time.

Barges… just across the water. Wisely or disastrously - it was hard to tell which - I went over and bought one.

Secunda the barge was called. There are lots of *Secunda*s in the Netherlands. It is the equivalent there of Smith or Patel; but she was striking nonetheless. A mighty thing by comparison with the boats of the English canals, she had a sleekness about her also, having once plied her trade under sail. Built of riveted steel, with a fine, sweeping prow, in her hull form she was not unlike the tea-clipper *Cutty Sark*. On her last trip in harness she carried 150 tons of coffee from Rotterdam to Utrecht.

The narrow boats of the English canals looked tiny by comparison. Those built for cargo could manage, generally, little more than twenty-five tons apiece. The *Arthur*, from the Leeds & Liverpool Canal, and twice the narrow boat size, carried maybe forty-five tons of coal when she was working. But the minimum the Dutch wished to establish was 300 tons. To them, *Secunda* was just another small barge.

A system of subsidies urged her operators to get the vessel out of trade. Only later did I realise that, in effect, the owners were receiving their money twice: once through the compensation the Netherlands state was paying, then again with the cash from me.

The search for a barge was enlivened on those cold winter days by push-starting the car of Jan, the man I employed as an agent, through the streets of Stavoren, up in Friesland. In the Netherlands at that time cars often ran on gas - that is if they did run, which was unlikely if the owner forgot to switch back to petrol before stopping the night before.

A morning routine developed, in which Jan and I sipped coffee together, crouched beside the stove in his little terraced house. There a list of prospective vessels would be brought to my attention, 'bargains', every one of them, however much the previous day's offerings had failed in that respect. Next I would scrape the ice off the windscreen while Jan failed to start his car. A spell of exercise followed, pushing, before some passer-by could be attracted to help and the motor fired up at last. Then, no longer in the state of mind for reasoned discussion, we set off to examine the latest of the semi-derelict tubs that Jan looked out in the mistaken belief that these were what I wanted.

It is easy now to make light of those experiences, to recall with a glow the streets of the old town, the row of gabled houses, many of them occupied by people from the barges. Covered in morning frost, the waterfront was a picture. Beyond lay the pastureland of Friesland, punctuated occasionally by farms amongst the wind-blown trees, unaltered in setting since the days of Ruisdael.

In reality I was frightened. What on Earth was I getting into? Could I afford it? Would this be another fantasy project, of which in boating there are many, in which a vessel becomes a soaker up of work, and money, and in the end comes to nought? Fortunately Jan was a better judge of barges than he was of motor-cars and, once he cottoned-on to the need to find a vessel of substance, we went down to Rotterdam to look at S*ecunda*.

As the priciest of all the craft that we saw, S*ecunda* would take most of the money I had; but at least she was well fitted-out. Her hull was not distorted through the carriage of scrap iron, or rotted by cement. Nor did she have one of those monumental engines, worthy of a place in a science museum. These were common in the older craft, massive, unwieldy things, in engine-rooms reminiscent of the dourest kind of chapel, adorned with giant spanners and other bothersome signs.

The price of the barge, of course, was merely the entry fee to an on-going, money-spending exercise. Her hold, at present a large empty space, would have to be fitted-out. Other expenses too, no doubt, would also be rearing their heads. So partners needed to be sought: folk, as yet unknown, who might be interested enough to put their own money down as well. To attract them an appealing vessel, well cared for at the outset, was absolutely vital.

They would have to be British, these people: the thought of rounding them up elsewhere was just too much. And so, inevitably,

Secunda would need to be moved to England, for enquirers there to look at, then hopefully take the plunge.

Stavoren is on the eastern shore of the Ijsselmeer, the fresh water lake that was once the Zuider Zee. Here in the bar-room, the décor of the ship's wheel on the wall and the photos of captains posed on the ice, were more than just tokens. Barging, still, was a central part of local life. There may have been a Girl Guide meeting at one end of the pub, but the circle of old geezers at the other, grouped strategically near the stove, had a fair percentage, according to Jan, of waterway retirees. In between lay in wait the grizzled fellow with a freighter out in the harbour who, disconcertingly, had only one ear. Babbling unintelligibly in deepest Friesian, he would sidle up to unburden himself, while the ham and eggs I had gone in there to eat went gradually cold. Maybe he was saying 'I do think Aldous Huxley was a little out of line when he wrote *Mortal Coils*' but somehow this was doubtful. As to the man in the bobble hat, stomping round the snooker table in his socks and shouting...

'The bank manager,' said Jan. 'Be careful with him. A tricky guy. You will need him when you buy your ship.'

Which was true. A pity he would not let me use the office phone. The public box down the street consumed money as if it were peanuts while the switchboards of England went about their duties. Insurance companies, in particular, with whom some kind of rapport was absolutely essential, seemed to be fuelled on low-level novocaine. 'Mr Blenkinsop? I think he's out at the moment ... Can anyone else help?' The flow of one-guilder coins kept the possibility open. 'Hold on a minute; I'll see if there's anything on his desk. What did you say your name was?'

Barges are not good at sea crossings. They blow sideways, their rudders get wafted in the swells, and they roll. When, several years beforehand, the *Arthur* made the journey round the coast from The Wash to the Thames, then, later, across the Channel to France, we experienced all of those things - and more. We were lucky with those voyages, darned lucky. And with *Secunda*, too, the gods were kind on the day. The weather was mild, mellowing to a glass-like calm. With me came Philip, the son of my friend and boatyard proprietor Michael Streat.

From Calais, which we got to through inland waterways, it was an 80 mile trip across the English Channel to Brownsworth, the village where *Secunda* would be kept. The sands of Essex gleamed in the evening sun as we threaded through the channels on the last of the incoming tide. Within the estuary, we were in shelter now. Here we could anchor in safety before going into Brownsworth in the morning. Instead of the neat clean waterways of the Netherlands, though, there was mud here, to a serious degree.

This was revealed when we got the anchor up again. The winch, a dreadful thing which we took it in turns to wind, brought in the cable link by painful link. Lots of mud came with it, stinky grey stuff that spattered us with spots. Weeks later it was still to be smelled in the bow, where the chain lived in an unsatisfactory kind of box. It revived strongly the memory of boiled Brussels sprouts while in digs as a student in Manchester.

A man rowed out from the boatyard at Brownsworth, to receive a well-soaked rope for his pains. Fortunately he clung onto this and after he had wrung out his trousers he began rowing again, to connect us with the shore.

Slowly now, *Secunda* edged forward into the creek, bumping from time to time as the waves came by, until she was secure in her berth. There was a shed on one side, an elderly sailing vessel on the other. Ahead were shacks with stove-pipe chimneys, and the wall of a pub. Beneath, to be revealed as the tide went out, was more of the same sticky mud.

When a vessel is up on the beach some of the pride in her dies. *Secunda* Enterprises, if there was to be such a body, would have to form up quickly, before despair set in.

The search for backers, long-winded and often disappointing, was conducted for much of the time from the office of *Waterways World.* Based in the brewing town of Burton-on-Trent, *Waterways World* was the gathering ground for those with a passion for canals. It was friends working there who, in those early days, provided me with employment. This was not as a journalist, since they had one of those already, in the shape of my friend Archy. Instead I was the odd-job man, the putter-up of shelves or a dasher down to the chemists in pursuit of photographic prints (the days of computers, unforeseen, were years yet into the future). It was work all the same, and I was grateful.

Archy, like myself, invested his future in the waterways. Out of a job himself once, he thought to start a magazine about them. No-one else was doing that, then. Canals were not so widely understood. With hearts in their mouths, Archy and three others set out on the great adventure.

It is difficult today, looking at the substantial, well-established magazine *Waterways World* has become, to register the uncertainty of its beginnings. Canal buffs across the nation, the group talked one another into believing, would be running to the newsagents, who in turn would be shouting into their telephones in search of extra copies. It was not to be. Of the thousands they printed, thousands made their way back - unsold.

There could be no other way but forward. This was something I would soon be finding myself. You can be trapped by a business idea. If you stop, you lose everything anyway. Freddie Laker, who long ago launched a cut-price airline - a novel and inspiring idea - was vilified after it collapsed for failing to warn those who were booking his flights that the business was in jeopardy. Had he done so, of course, it would have crashed there and then.

Archy and his pals - though they were not such pals by then - had no other option but to plunge ever onwards; and an extremely dicey plunge this was. The magazine, launched as a quarterly into a market that was, to put it kindly, extremely thin, moved now into monthly publication. If they did not do this, they had learned, W H Smith was not prepared to look at them. Those who could do so out of Archy's team blandished the bank manager with the deeds of their houses - a hideously risky procedure for which a strong moral case can be made for having it banned. But, again, they had to. Their company, which already owed the printers a packet, would otherwise have collapsed.

They survived, then prospered, to the extent that Mr Newton Husbands, the kindly soul who rented them the larger part of the property from which he ran his brewing business, was reduced, over the months, to occupying the tiniest portion himself. Meanwhile Archy and his partners expanded into the rest, choking the stairway with packages and the latest in books for mail-order. Somewhere under those stairs Mr Newton Husbands battled on with the threat, ever-present, that the floor above might collapse under the sheer weight of paper. His appearances, which were intermittent and unexpected, had the knack of taking people by surprise. Newcomers could be found wondering who he was.

In the office the atmosphere was matey. 'They're never in, these buggers, are they?' cried Russ the advertisement manager while on the phone about some copy, 'Oh… Is that Mr Carter?'

Betweentimes he would help frame little notices to put in the 'Business Opportunities' column.

'French canals,' these began, going on to refer to 'a canal holiday barge' for which a 'proposed company' needed 'additional capital.'

France was now confirmed, although the Netherlands, familiar through *Secunda*, still held an appeal. A straw poll of relatives soon put this right. Wine, sunshine, good food, amiable peasantry in overalls - these were the associations with France. Holland, by comparison, mustered clogs, tulips, fingers in dykes, Vincent Van Gogh - though he did much of his work in France anyway, didn't he? - and unexciting cheese.

France it was going to be, and the Canal du Nivernais probably, the dramatic if neglected route on the western side of Burgundy where, a summer or two before, Richard had been wondering about his cook. There was also in this region the lure of the vineyards in and around Chablis, although, as a canal obsessive rather than a wine one, that did not attract me greatly. The trend towards reversing those interests had yet to come.

As a break from the office routine, Archy and I would review a narrow boat occasionally, craft derived from the old working type, but with cabins and comforts on board. Always we would be late on these journeys, burdened as we were by the commissions from Russ: maps for the shop at Musing-on-Cherwell or a call, if we would, on the Fazackerly brothers at Major's End to remind them to pay their bloody bill.

Dusk would be nigh by the time that we reached the boat, to discover a message from the builder who, abandoning his plan to take us out to lunch, still felt it proper to explain how the gas system worked. We would fiddle about with keys then tumble into the saloon at last, bearing our cargo of maps, still undelivered, printer's proofs to be read and returned, somehow, the following morning and the piles of reader's letters, review copies for the books pages, or notices about tax.

As senior boat examiner present, Archy had the first choice of bed. Then, getting our priorities right, we inspected the privy. This essential area of the boat, looming large in the future of my business career, was referred to privately as the Talking Cupboard, the flimsiness of its walls allowing the occupant to continue in normal conversation with those sitting in the saloon.

English narrow boats presented little variation at the time. There were rare and honourable exceptions but, because the locks they pass through are thin, the arrangement in a narrow boat has to be linear: saloon, galley, Talking Cupboard, cabins; or later, as a design breakthrough, saloon, galley, cabins, Talking Cupboard and an area for hanging up raincoats. Fittings varied little. Lighting, for instance, because of a dependence on batteries, was generally from fluorescent tubes, with the aura, sometimes, of an out-patient's waiting room.

There was also, because of the shortage of space, an arrangement called a 'dinette', whereby, after fiddling with its supports, the table could be lowered to fill the gap between the seating and turn itself into a bed. It was the dinette usually to which I was consigned, with the disadvantages of that arrangement, in which the cushions drifted apart during the night and Archy, who got up earlier than I did, wanting the space for his breakfast. Aboard the *Secunda*, I found myself vowing, there would be no dinettes.

After several of these outings our enthusiasm for the vessel under review related directly to the quietness of the engine. This could vary, from a tolerable bumbling hum, through the level of a bus struggling into the Alps, to a barking roar that was quite insupportable. So great was the din on one occasion that we took to travelling as fast as we decently could, before switching off for a spell, to glide in tranquillity before starting once again. We asked the builder to put these matters right then invited him to give us a call, but he went bust in the meantime.

Going bust. Folk in the boat business appeared to do this often. It was worrying. Or half-worrying, for, while guessing that the *Secunda* project could provide a bumpy ride, some notion of luck still hung about. We would make it, wouldn't we? The cautionary joke of the man falling from the Empire State Building saying 'So far, so good,' came back from time to time. But, soon enough, it got pushed aside. Disaster, surely, could never happen with *Secunda*? Somehow, it would all work out.

Person wanted, of romantic inclination, with Five Thousand Pounds to risk on a dodgy project. Ability to sit through long, meandering meetings without contradicting anyone a definite advantage. No time-wasters, please.

This is what the advertisement should have been saying; but, of course, it could not. Instead, a serious business venture was promoted. Those who wrote received in return a copy of the drawings my brother had prepared for conversion of the vessel, together with an exposition by myself and a series of cash-flows.

Cash-flow projections aim to show the financial future. It took a little time to learn how to do them, with the aid of the man who, at the end of it all, would become our accountant. Once grasped, though, cash-flows were easy. You simply guessed your expenses each month on food, employment and the like, then imagined the income to cover them. The only serious drawback, in those days before word processors, was the boredom of typing them out.

The backers, or the potential ones, began to respond to the advertisements. Conjuring up, as the term 'backer' does, the vision of an impresario in an overcoat, it was a surprise to discover what a mixed bunch they were. There would be five, on average, for each issue of *Waterways World*. Of these, as it turned out, three at least would generally be poorer than I was. Absence of money, however, did not deter the curious from getting in touch; many an evening was spent typing out letters to them, with estimates of cost and - even more rashly - of profits to be made.

It was often with Bob, who had already volunteered a share in the project, that I met these respondees. Bob, a friend from way back, was working in insurance. Meeting people was central to his trade. By wearing a suit on these outings, one that actually fitted, he brought us credibility.

It was his geniality that broke the ice, while I, nervous at what we were proposing, usually tended to stumble. We met all sorts: canal enthusiasts who 'liked the idea of it' but had no cash, a woman breeder of fox terriers who turned our discussion into a rant against the rules concerning the importation of animals, and a series of hard-nosed gentlemen in the motor, timber and oil-prospecting trades.

These last, while professing a co-operative spirit, would plainly only have been happy had they sat at the head of the table. 'It's no good treating this as fun,' one said emphatically. 'This is a business, and it's got to be run as a business.' But, in truth, he would be in it because he thought it might be fun. Whether he himself would be fun, of course, was another matter.

Who, Bob and I would ask ourselves, might we be meeting next? Personalised number plates were a worrying sign. So, in that era before credit cards became common, was the gold-coloured one from American Express. It did not do to be flashy, we felt. Barges did not fit in with that.

With the money all tied up in the vessel, my own shortage of cash bore heavily. Sometimes, when those coming looked as compatible as cats in a cage of canaries, the temptation still remained to sit them down and get them to write out a cheque. As the bank balance continued to teeter, Attila the Hun, at times, would have been welcome. In the end, with the exception of Luke, who was introduced by a pal down at Brownsworth, and the latest newcomer, Hector, everyone who joined was known to me already.

Hector arrived by way of the ad. A letter from Saudi Arabia sealed the deal. If that sounds grand it is merely that *Waterways World* reached overseas readers and Hector was one of those. After teaching English in Riyadh he was now coming home, bringing his family with him. Home was in the Cumbrian hills. Bob and I went to track Hector down, at the end of a mountain path. It was as far from Burgundy as we ever looked likely to get.

Once we arrived and had a cup of tea, Bob went out of the house again to bring something from his car. A squadron of hens had settled on its roof, while a goat was standing with its forelegs on the bonnet, as if it were a mechanic trying to get in. Hector was the man for us. Our team was complete.

2: IN BUSINESS

From then on it was serious. In that office in London where the charwoman cast her shadow, the eight of us signed things. There were shares to be issued, articles to approve, the need for motions to be passed. It was as if we knew what we were doing. I now became a company director, the Managing Director in fact. By accident, also, I seemed to be Chairman as well. Neither of these honorifics, as it turned out, would prevent the others from hi-jacking a meeting when they felt like it; but at least it provided a role now that would merit me a wage.

Directorship ... what a thought. It was flattering to become such a high-ranking officer, even if the only previous contact with the species had been in the papers. 'Simon Whatsisname,' a news item would say, 'Company Director, appeared before magistrates today, accused of driving under the influence of drink/rioting at a football match/making off with the Round Table funds.'

With the formalities of the meeting over we agreed to retire, before hypothermia set in, to the lounge of a hotel in Park Lane. There, with gentlemen in Arab costume hovering in the background because we had taken all the chairs, we looked at the designs for *Secunda* again. Luke, who would be doing the work on the boat, listed the materials he would be needing; Betty, who was generous, and without whom nothing would have happened at all, was anxious to review the interior. Others exchanged boating anecdotes.

From across the room a pair of smartly-dressed Japanese, no doubt concerned with ore carriers, or the movement of an automobile empire from one continent to the next, looked on with interest as the designs were unrolled. My brother, who was also in the group, had carefully drawn these up, showing how, with a bit of enterprise, the hold of our barge could be fitted with cabins, galley and a saloon. After that, we reckoned, we would be cruising into France with *un bateau par excellence*.

This is the best bit of business: the making of fanciful plans before the money trickles away and anxiety sets in. That evening, to celebrate getting so far, my girl-friend Portia and I went to a restaurant round the corner. There, in anticipation of the association with France now to be renewed, we had snails in garlic butter sauce.

The Shareholders were a mixed group, some of them wealthy - 'comfortable', as they liked to put it - some less so. Betty, whose husband was Sales Director of the family furniture firm, contributed £5,000, increasing this later to £10,000 as the budget over-ran. My elder brother Peter had just a £1 share, with the complicated promise of more, once his design work was done.

My own shareholding, of around £7,000, represented the value of *Secunda* before the conversion work began. Changes in the exchange rate had pushed this figure up. The European Community, as today it is called, was a looser arrangement then. Britain, indeed, had only recently joined. Trade barriers remained in place. Separate currencies were maintained. The purchase price of the barge in Holland, at 30,000 guilders, amounted to £4,700 when *Secunda* was found - somewhere around the annual salary of the editor of a boating magazine at that time, to put such a sum in perspective. But the Pound was on the slide and in the end - in terms of Sterling - the vessel cost a great deal more.

Those funny little tables in the financial pages of the newspapers took on new meaning. So also, before bringing the boat to England, did the realisation that Bank of England permission needed to be sought in sending any money abroad. There were rules about this - though nothing about getting on with it. While the Pound fell remorselessly, those in the authorisation division of the Bank of England (whose office, mysteriously, appeared to be in Glasgow) would be wandering around looking for something to sharpen their quills with. I have scarcely forgiven them, even now.

I had put the cost of the venture at £30,000. It was a terrifying miscalculation. £57,000 was the total in the end. To this several weighty borrowings had to be added as reality tightened its grip. And one pound then was worth more than five in 2009.

The *Secunda*, while backers were being sought, sat quietly in the creek in Essex. Gradually, over the months, her paint lost its glow. Muddy footprints invaded the deck while the hatches, which were of wood, were starting to rot at the edges. Such things happen to boats. From smartness to infirmity is but a few swift strides. The spell of immobility had been quite long enough.

Spruceness is not a characteristic of the Essex boating centres. There is too much muck around for that. Potent skies brood over a long, low shoreline. Geese flap by. Men in oilskins sniff the air, then retire indoors for further brews of tea. The homecoming yachtsman arrives, dragging up to the slipway a dinghy loaded with his family. Over their clothes, in their kit and on their hair, is a spattering of mud.

Yachting, when people want it to be, can be considered luxurious. There are the sun-drenched bays of the Aegean or Caribbean, where cocktails may be consumed on the after deck - as they are at Monte or in the Seychelles. An alternative view, but equally romantic, is that of hardiness, of storms being weathered, the Nelson-inspired notion of sea-doggery. Seasoned old salts haul on the mainsheet, spitting with disdain at the storm.

It was the latter of these images that Brownsworth embraced. Smocks, beards and square-rigged trousers appeared to be the currency here. The Thames Sailing Barge was a major inspiration, the work-horse in the great days of trade out of London's river. None of them nowadays performs such tasks; but there survive a number of these vessels, restored as steam locomotives sometimes are, at an expense that is staggering. Like the cargo-carrying narrow boats of the English canals they still have an aura about them, of readiness for action, commissions to be fulfilled.

Thereafter, in order of admiration, were gaff-rigged fishing smacks and yachts built out of wood; to be followed, at a distance, by anything else with sails on. Only after that came craft under power.

In circles such as these, where to enter a pub was like playing a bit part in *Mutiny on the Bounty*, a vessel such as *Secunda* stood a long way down the list, although, as I took care to explain, she had long ago been propelled by wind-power alone. We also gathered points, it turned out, by virtue of the journey from Calais. For, despite all the talk in the *Concertina and Spittoon* and its rival *The Robber's Revenge*, the habit of voyaging abroad - 'going foreign' as it was termed - was not that common. Such trips as were made tended to be lingered over, rather as people recalled their adventures in the armed forces, or the distant days of youth.

You either went to *The Robber's* or the *Concertina*, but not to both, for there was a rivalry between them that sometimes broke into fights. The causes of these disputes seemed usually to be domestic, although the occasional nautical matter intruded. How did that scoundrel So-and-So get a mooring by the quay? Everyone knew there was a waiting list!

A serious-looking woman came into the pub one evening. 'Could you tell me where I might find the *Grantham Belle*,' she asked in tones that brooked no idle chat.

The Landlord was caught off his guard. 'I can give them a message,' he stuttered, looking rather sheepish.

'Tell the Captain his wife is waiting to see him,' the visitor declared.

'Oh,' said the Landlord, before he could stop himself; 'but the Captain's wife is already on board!'

This is the stuff of sailing, the nitty-gritty of life on the water. Going back through the boatyard shed that evening, pausing but briefly to disentangle the handle of a vice that had caught in the pocket of my trousers, I reflected with Portia on the place in which we found ourselves. You had to keep moving at Brownsworth. Otherwise you got stuck there, glued, so to speak, in the mud.

It was at Brownsworth that Luke joined our circle. Luke was a farmer, and a local farmer too, with a liking for boats. Thankfully, he kept outside the Brownsworth milieu, mooring his own vessel elsewhere. Amazingly also, he was prepared to convert the *Secunda* for us, and not for cash directly, but in exchange for shares.

A drawback to this arrangement was having to yield to Luke's ideas, some of which were doubtful. Big in stature, big in business, used to having his own way, Luke was a difficult man to stop; but, on the plus side, he did get the thing built, which until then had seemed unlikely.

To mention a farmer is to conjure up the notion of haystacks, yokels throwing seed out of bags. It was not like that. Luke had fields certainly, positive prairies in fact. Over these, mighty machines worked their way. There were silos and barns, concentration camps for pigs, houses for the staff, all of which had to be maintained. A multi-skilled workforce did this: electricians, plumbers and carpenters amongst them. Several of these, under Luke's aegis, would now be working for us.

It was this highly drilled team that, once the whistle was blown, descended upon *Secunda* like an army of warrior ants. First of all they poured tons of concrete into the hold. There, thanks to the skill Luke had with concrete, it set with the consistency of granite. This was confirmed a year or two later when I tried to dig some out again. It was not a bad idea in theory, for as well as providing a floor for the cabins it ballasted the vessel down; and we needed that, or so we thought, to get beneath the bridges of the canals we were going to travel.

Concrete nowadays is a no-no in France and was regarded with suspicion even then; but our notion of Authority across the Channel verged upon the derisory. On the English canals at the time there were no rules whatsoever. Why should France be different? And even if it was we surely could wangle our way along? Like other doubtful propositions, the concrete was agreed to at our meetings in *Secunda*'s aft cabin. There, with the stove roaring and the oxygen sufficiently depleted to addle the keenest commercial brain, a lot was said that would later be regretted,

Guy Fawkes Night intervened. Always a source of entertainment in the neighbourhood, the action that year was of a particularly passionate nature. The Firework Fund had gone walkabout. 'This money is not to pay for drinks at committee meetings,' a purple-faced figure was heard shouting at the inn. Fisticuffs followed and, as a result, two celebrations were held that year. One had the fireworks, such as there were, the other an enormous bonfire. Set for territorial reasons so close to *The Robber's Revenge* that it blistered the paintwork; the blaze cracked several windows as well.

'Where are our sawing trestles?' Luke's carpenters asked the next day; but it was too late. *Secunda*'s nameboard seemed likewise to have disappeared. Handsomely carved in Dordrecht many years before, it had rashly been left ashore for some scavenger to gather.

On the morning after the bonfire, Luke's squad were the only ones working. For the rest of Brownsworth it was hangover time. Wisps of smoke could be seen curling from the shacks on the foreshore while the occupants, no doubt, dreamed of voyages to Antigua, or plotted against rivals in love.

In short order a superstructure was created over the hold area, faithfully following the drawings. It had been put there while the householders of Shore Street - one of several distinctive factions in Brownsworth society - were grumbling still about the concrete lorries.

By now other entrepreneurs appeared to be entering the game. A team of people, we learned, was beavering away at Brightlingsea with a vessel similar to our own. No expense was being spared there (this was according to the barmaid at the *Concertina and Spittoon,* so the information had yet to be verified).

There was a young architect from Birmingham, Chris Ryle, who had rescued the *Pisgah*, previously used for carrying grain into the

Warwickshire Avon, and something of an iconic vessel in those parts. Fitting out *Pisgah* with his Dad, he had, with commendable bravery, made the journey past Lands End to Le Havre, then up the Seine to Paris.

Then there was Stanley. Stanley was a New Yorker, the classic rich American of folklore, or so it was said. It was Archy who told us of him, with the news that Stanley was preparing, not just one, but a veritable fleet of these craft. By the sound of things no expense was being spared by him either.

Stanley himself was a buoyant, bonhomous fellow. We were to meet him briefly when he came to Brownsworth to pass the conventional pleasantries. What he really made of us I cannot imagine, for the league he played in was different to our own.

He made his money, it emerged, on the futures market - a knife-edged activity in which electronic gadgets were beginning to appear, little hand-held screens that enabled people such as Stanley to take the prices to bed with them, or prop them beside his plate while chewing on his lunch. It was flattering in a way to think such a high-powered tycoon should be tempted into the same kind of business as our own.

Stanley's UK camp was over at Worcester, where two substantial barges had already arrived, brought by heroes unsung all the way from mainland Europe. It would be an idea, it was now decided, for me to go and see them, to consolidate the connection.

Stanley, it was thought, should be enrolled as an ally. He was American after all, and it was Americans, we were beginning to gather, we ought to be appealing to most. Richard and his colleagues, certainly, drew the bulk of their clients from the USA. Maybe, to simplify our lives a little, Stanley could hand us any customers he happened to have spare.

It was incredibly naïve of us to have thought like that. We were still in a dream world here, with a near-fatal assumption that enough willing travellers would be stooging around to satisfy us all. Filling the barge with passengers, to our way of thinking, was merely a matter of hoisting the flag, then watching folk walk up the gangplank. When you open a shop, after all, people stroll past the door and some come inside.

As a gesture, I found an operator of self-drive hire boats in England who was prepared to be our agent, to look out for customers and to collect the money from them. While they would sell our holidays through the routine processes to which they were accustomed, we could, possibly, produce some handouts to periodicals and place the odd small ad. But that was all. We saw little need to do much else.

Travelling to Worcester one day, I found Stanley's two craft lying on the Severn, one of the very few waterways in England of sufficient size to take them. Disappointingly, neither Stanley, nor his wife Jarrett, was there. Preoccupied with something called 'promotion', they were back in the USA, but a message of welcome allowed me to root around.

The larger of the craft was the *Janine*, the saloon of which, at first brush, was the size of a billiard hall. There was lots of teak about, while the engine-room, a warren of generators, vacuum pumps and so forth, positively hummed with, well, … money.

Then there were the lavatories. Each cabin had one. If this sounds obvious today, it was not the fashion those years ago. 'It cannot be done' was the mantra, and all the other craft that we knew, save those belonging to the mega-rich in the Mediterranean, had WC cubicles that were shared. It was a boating convention. Even our recent Prime Minister, Edward Heath, when he went ocean racing in his trophy-winning *Morning Cloud*, crouched, as did all of his crew (in turn, rather than collectively) in the single, tiny compartment. The newspapers and satirical publications tried to make something of this; but, on boats, it was explained to them, that was how things were.

On the English canals WCs were still the same worrying things as Archy and I experienced, boxed in a plywood compartment. On yachts there was a kind with taps and levers, instruments of torment, from which, as a development, there was an electrified version, with which you pushed on a button to operate the pump, then ran away. On *Secunda* we were installing three of these, in cubicles standing in a row.

Stanley on the other hand was starting with what the customers wanted - one for each cabin. Vacuum-operated, there were connections through a maze of pipes to a whacking great pump in the engine-room. 'They're the same as they have on Concorde,' one of the workforce stated proudly as I checked the vessel over. And there they were, looking every bit as usable as those on a supersonic flight.

95% of the people who came on barges, it was to prove, could hardly tell a bollard from a standard lamp nor why, on reaching a lock, we did not simply open the gates at each end then cruise straight through. But there were certain items they expected, as necessary as the cutlery on the table or a roof above their heads. Leading this list was 'private facilities,' a shower and WC with each cabin. This, for the vast majority of enquirers, was what they required first of all. That there were practical difficulties in providing such a service concerned them not the slightest.

Later we were to learn what Stanley's WCs would be costing; then felt a little better. Likewise came the discovery that they, or the pumps on which they depended, were not immune to the extraordinary things people dropped into them. The image is conjured up of a seething group of passengers battering on doors with 'Out of Order' written on them as Concorde winged its way to New York. That those flights were quick could have been their saving. None of the customers for barges, on the other hand, would have been prey to such doubts before they put their money down and booked.

'He's got sixteen fellers working on just the one boat,' I reported back at Brownsworth. 'God knows how many on the other. Big cabins, a saloon five times the size of ours. And the lavatories ...'

The *Janine* would be running from Dijon, near where the wine area began, to Lyon, which had one of the most prestigious restaurants in France. A meal would be taken there each week. Arrangements were also being made for someone who knew about such things to escort people to vineyards on the way.

There were scraps of encouragement to be drawn here, for the waterways on that route, as I knew, were monotonous and impersonal. There was the canal from Dijon, so direct it could have been drawn with a ruler, descending lock after repetitive lock into the wide, flat valley of the Saône. No longer at that point was the river such an alluring stream as where the man in the Citroën once provided a lift. Here, having been enlarged for freight on a grand scale, it was a straightened watercourse. Such sights as existed were largely at a distance, fading into the haze.

I was in denial here, really. Beaune, Clos De Vougeot, and Gevrey-Chambertin lay along this route - or sufficiently close for a motor-coach to get there - and the resonance of those names would be pulling the customers in. Stanley did not seek canal enthusiasts after all.

The others in our group also affected to be unimpressed. 'Clichéd tourist stuff,' they said. 'It's a different market'. Our own trips would be natural, exploratory holidays, conducted in a spirit of mutual adventure on waterways with variety. We were whistling in the dark, of course, and should have known better.

By this stage most of the post consisted of bills. There were bills for plywood, bills for sinks and taps, bills, bills and more bills. It did not need an ace financier to realise the sums were not adding up. 'Stop, stop' I felt like shouting at a meeting as one of our number, befuddled by the stove again, suggested we consult the Bluffbody Brothers of Chirpington, designers of kitchens for the gentry. Swift action was needed here. So, before the lobby gathered steam, I located through the pages of *Exchange & Mart* a knowing gentleman in Hackney who sold us a second-hand range. 'That's a good cooker that one is,' he advised while agreeing, for a further consideration, to bring it over on his truck. 'Do you many a good Coq Au Vin.'

Meanwhile, as our money trickled away, I worked up a scheme with the local bank manager whereby, in exchange for Joint and Several Guarantees, he would lend us what was needed to finish the job. It was a critical interview; Bob not being around I would have to put on the show on my own. Wearing a suit for such meetings was nigh-on essential in those times: Marks & Spencer sold suits at £69.99, and if mine made me look like Cornelius the Elephant in the Barbar stories, it boosted my confidence enough to extol the soundness and credibility of the captains of industry with whom the project was surrounded.

Blinking at the cash-flows - into which, in the typewriting equivalent of the Freudian slip, the red part of the ribbon had partially strayed - the manager at the bank looked bothered for a while, then surprised me by making this offer. For the rest of the day I felt elated.

The captains of industry, alas, when they were consulted, would not play ball. Joint and Several Guarantees, as they pointed out, meant any one of them could be liable for the entire sum, if or when things went wrong. 'But the bank says it's normal,' I stuttered. 'Maybe,' came the reply, 'but it isn't normal to us.'

Instead, we could raise a lesser amount by putting the boat herself down as security. It was only £8,000 the bank would be giving us for this, as opposed to the twenty-odd grand that we needed, but it delayed, at least, the visit to the insolvency practitioners.

Amongst the hoops to be gone through now was getting *Secunda* registered, in order to satisfy the bank. For this the papers would have to be translated. Only then could we approach the Registrar of Shipping in Cardiff. For the translation part I found a Dutchman in Whitechapel, for whom, he said, it made an agreeable change to his involvement in Anglo-Flemish divorce. Then came Measurement, for which someone on an approved list would look the vessel over. The list itself, which was lengthy, was an unexpected mixture of private companies and specialised government departments. That there were hazards in this became apparent very soon.

'Mister Liley,' came the voice down the phone. 'Department of Trade here. About this barge of yours … Which I have been to see …' *Merde alors*! When sticking a pin in the list I had landed on the particular government outfit that considered itself the police force for shipping. Measurement was only one of its tasks. The others, mainly, involved the application of the rules.

Measurement, as required by the Registrar, was one of the weirdest matters in the syllabus. Crew areas, ship's stores and the space for machinery played a positive or deductive role, or did not matter at all, depending on whether it was Gross, Registered, Displacement or Deadweight Tonnage we were talking about. The function of the vessel also made a difference and when, without thinking, I put down 'passenger-carrying on the French canals', the alarm bells went off.

Had I written 'motor yacht' instead there would have been no trouble at all. We could have taken *Secunda* out to sea without official hindrance then drowned ourselves. 'Passengers', though, were a different matter (I have never understood the logic of this: you can, in many activities, take your friends or family out and threaten their lives, but not if they pay).

The people I had been to see about Registration, deprived of other things to do by the exodus of shipping from London during that era, were in no mood to take *Secunda* lightly. They had an office in Seething Lane, which should have been a warning.

It was entirely a coincidence that the initial visit of the measuring man, made while I was tussling with a broken-down van filled with bedframes out on the Mile End Road, coincided with the application of varnish to the ceiling of our new saloon. As a consequence of this Luke's team leader, a small and diligent Welshman who was working from the top of a ladder, started to sing. Then, as the fumes became stronger, he was seen to be wobbling on his perch. Rescued by his companions, he was dragged outside for a breather - just as the measuring man arrived.

The sight of this trio reeling about in the open air may have bolstered the suspicion that in a number of ways we were not quite up to it. As one of the workforce said later, 'he did seem a bit put out.' (not least, possibly, because the visitor was told in the robustest of terms to go and get lost, though the gang became evasive when pressed on this point).

The list of non-compliances was considerable. 'Use of unapproved materials, insufficient intermediate bulkheads, certification of personnel unavailable ...' It was a depressing phone call that day. Getting back across the Channel, it seemed, would now be a problem.

'You'll need a Loadline Exemption Certificate,' the voice continued. 'And with a vessel like that you'll never get one.'

Archy once told me that on some boat trip we conducted together, in the times of full employment, I sat up in the night to shout 'Trade Descriptions Act' at the top of my voice, before crashing back onto my bunk again. This happened shortly after I became the editor of a boating magazine myself, as the responsibility in that role for everything that was printed, including the wilder claims of our advertisers, began to sink in. Now Loadline Exemption Certificates, seemingly, were looming as a replacement.

'She'll have to go as a dead tow,' the man said. 'It's the only way.'

A dead tow meant being pulled across the Channel by a tug - as chancy a business as going without one, since the captains of tugs are not inclined to hang about. If the weather is bad on the day, or even mediocre, the damage inflicted by being thumped through the waves can be enormous.

The cost of this doubtful experience was, we already knew, around £6,000. Another Dutch barge had appeared off Brownsworth a week or two beforehand, astern of an ocean-going tug several sizes larger than herself. Being towed in this fashion - through, rather than over, the Channel's rolling seas - she had lost her wheelhouse. Lots of other things on board got smashed up as well, the experience providing several night's gossip in the waterside pubs. We seemed to be in a circular situation here, in which to borrow £8,000 a process had to be gone through in which three-quarters of that total went out of the window for starters, to be followed, probably, by damage to the vessel herself.

It seemed a good idea not to explode down the telephone. 'Fine,' I managed to say. 'We were thinking of doing that anyway.'

'Fine,' said the caller in return. 'I'll come along and see your ship again, and we can go through the arrangements.' His fee per visit, he said, was £72, marginally more than the cost of that suit.

One of the projects on board was the construction of a freezer. The idea of this, imaginative in its conception, disastrous in execution, was that, as the main engine turned, it should also drive a compressor. From this, in theory, great coldness would result.

The freezer itself was a mighty chest with a top-opening lid. It was this I found the measuring man peering into when next he came on board. Briefly, I considered severing the string that held it open, but, with relations so delicate, decided to introduce myself instead. He was bearded, in Government-issue windcheater, with a spiel of explanation as to his role. 'Necessary to maintain standards' seemed to be a part of it.

'Don't look at me like that.' he next declared. 'If you don't like it you can write to your MP.' It seemed a well-rehearsed line. I managed a dutiful smile.

'See if he collects something …' a friend had suggested.

'Collects?'

'Yes. Find out what it is. Postage stamps, Toby jugs, things like that. They often do, these people. It's a weakness. Part of the make-up. Give it a try anyway. Might do the trick.'

Pondering these words I followed the measuring man round the ship while he thought of things to do. Boarding up the windows was an obvious one, bracing the rudder with chains something we could do without. After half an hour of this the conversation turned towards the cargo vessels from Scandinavia that he inspected, which, when transferred to British registry, had to have their safety gear thrown away. Life-jackets, extinguishers, rockets and radios: all came to be scrapped because they were not on some British-approved list.

'A shame really,' he said, 'because it's such good stuff. Better than ours actually. But there you are.' As he was wearing dark glasses it was difficult to tell if he was being sarcastic, but he sounded quite serious to me.

The question of the tug arose and I said it was being thought about. 'Good,' he responded. 'By the way, do you want those empty bottles over there? No? Mind if I have them? Collect them,' he explained. 'Put plum wine in them.' Clinking under his load, he departed, mellowed perhaps by his acquisition. Would he be coming again though? Would he be checking out the tug? A deep unease remained.

We had our launching party that May and enough people came to have made us a profit, had they all been customers.

The latter, alas, despite some ads in a magazine and a mailshot, were in very short supply. While Stanley's two great barges, the *Janine* and her sister ship *Linquenda*, were solidly booked already, the numbers joining us each week could be counted on the fingers, and sometimes the thumbs, of one hand.

'There's a lot of activity in the market place,' our narrow boat agent reported, in the jargon of his trade. It is the nature of these people to be buoyant, but buoyancy is not the same as bookings.

Don't worry,' Portia said. 'They'll come.' But they didn't, and it was worrying

In the short term, though, setting off for France took priority.

3: INTO FRANCE

In order to move down the creek, to somewhere deep enough for ocean-going tugs to get at, *Secunda* was allowed to proceed under her own power. Even the Department of Trade accepted that. Indeed, in his bottle-collecting manifestation, its representative no longer seemed so concerned. To my huge relief, since I contrived to arrange our departure for a Saturday, his zeal was sufficiently diminished for him not to be around.

This was just as well since, once we got to the rendezvous point, no such tug turned up. Someone had completely failed to arrange it. It must have been me. The alternative for us, of course, was to have been ruined.

People ask how long it took to cross to Calais. The answer: an emotional eternity. To be out in a less-than-seaworthy vessel, when all depends on the weather, preys heavily on the imagination; especially without such back-ups as ship-to-shore radio, which was expensive at the time. Having said that, there was no alternative but to do it.

Helping on this trip were Owen, taking a break from the local bookshop, and Frank. Frank was a proper captain, on leave from a shipping company, who cannot have realised what he was getting into. To his credit he stayed the course. This was vital because Owen, though an experienced yachtsman, was not experienced enough to have detected at ankle-height a cable across the floor in Brownsworth's well-known shed. With an arm in plaster and braced across his chest he was some way short of being able-bodied, but he did keep up morale, doing his stint at the wheel and even preparing scrambled egg.

On the *Secunda* a major area of worry lay in the system Harry S., one of Luke's contractors, had installed for the freezer, a whirling medley of belts and pumps that somehow embraced the main engine cooling. Already on a trial run this caused difficulties, but Harry had plunged into the engine-room and fixed all that, or so he said. While I had cleared the fuel tanks of gunge - wherein the majority of problems lie with motor craft at sea - the belt system was more uncertain. With the threat of the measuring man's visits still in mind, and a favourable forecast for the day, only the briefest of tests could be undergone. Risky though it was, and unprofessional, Harry's word would have to be taken.

In the days when I helped to deliver yachts, a term encompassing everything from greyhounds of the sea to the most appalling deathtraps, there was a particular expression we learned to be wary of. As people at a shipyard, whether in Cannes or Newcastle-on-Tyne, struggled with a gearbox or patched up the rigging of a ketch some way past her prime, a terrible phrase would spring from their lips. What they really wanted to say was 'Dunno. Bit of a mystery this. Maybe it's alright, maybe it's not. Either way, why don't these people just piss off?' What they said instead was 'You'll be alright when you get to sea.'

As we manoeuvred the *Secunda* away from Brownsworth, Harry S came down to the jetty to see us off. 'Are you sure about those belts, Harry?' I shouted. 'You'll be alright when you get to sea,' came the reply, and I knew we had problems. Had he the courage of his convictions to have come to sea with us I could happily have killed him, though bearing in mind his interest in the martial arts and his being twice the size that I was, it would have been a close-run thing.

Sure enough, half an hour later, the belts began to slip and burn. As we were still in shelter, there remained a chance to fix them. Anchoring was called for. As Frank and I capered around the fore-deck and Owen waved his plastered arm, the winch suddenly released itself in a blur of whirling handles, putting out a quantity of heavy chain. We found this when we came to wind it in again, but by then the belts had been removed. We would have to do without the various things they were driving, but at least we were mobile again. Fortunately no promoters of tugs rowed out to confront us, and the rest of the voyage, conducted once more in blessed calm, lasted a further fourteen hours.

Others may talk cheerfully of taking such vessels to and from the Continental shore, and there is a growing body that do. Even narrow boats have crossed; so too did the *Arthur*, grotesquely unseaworthy as she was in several particular ways; but I have never liked these trips. The hours of waiting beforehand; the scuffles with suspect equipment; the off-watch periods, supposedly spent sleeping, though all the while listening to the engine; the recording of forecasts and the wondering whether to put into Ramsgate and face officialdom there: these, and more, make purgatory of the journey. When your savings hang upon the venture it winds the tension up further.

I am not proud of that voyage, which depended too much on luck; but we were well into risk-taking by then.

The customs officers at Calais reacted strongly to Frank. It was the stamps in his passport that did it, magnificent illuminated things some of them, bearing names such as Pusan or Macao, though how they might be connected with a barge staggering over from England remained unclear.

'These people mean business,' murmured Owen, as two gentlemen in uniform prised open the panels in Frank's cabin. Severely, they demanded to know what lay beyond the surfaces they exposed. The answer, 'the water in the harbour,' drew hurt looks; so they turned instead to pursing their lips at our liquor supply.

There was a burly one who looked like Oliver Hardy and a small, slight chap who could have been Stan Laurel, though it was difficult to tell with jokes in such short supply. Only gradually did we realise they were padding out time until the lunch break. At which, after solemnly sealing up some drink in a cupboard - the left-overs from our launching party - they professed themselves satisfied then slipped away down the quay.

It was an early brush with a group that would torment me seriously in times to come. Customs officials are not confined simply to the ports. They pop up in many places, certainly in France, including, it would prove, beside the canals. But, tempting though it is to say what a lot of rotters French Customs could be, they let us off favourably here. In Britain, vessels were liable to import duty at a swingeing 25% - save for those 'not adapted for recreation or pleasure', an intriguing acceptance that you can have one without the other. *Secunda*, unconverted on arrival at Brownsworth, fortunately filled that bill. So, after a blood-curdling encounter with a man in a pressed white shirt, I had been able to wriggle out of it.

Happily, in France the opposite applied. Only vessels actively in trade would be liable, while the rest could be left - as often in

France - to be dealt with some other day. Eventually we would be made to pay, and the duty could be large; but in France, a land of postponements, there was a breathing space still.

Free now to make our way farther south, we did so without hindrance - as far as the second bridge on the canal out of Calais. There, despite all the concrete on board, our wheelhouse was still too high.

Massively constructed in hardwood, this considerable structure could, in theory, be dismantled had not the Mudde Family, *Secunda*'s previous owners, in the Dutch obsession with varnish, managed to encapsulate its fitments in a rugged kind of amber. There were hinges and wires, the mechanism for a hooter, all of them sealed, not to say embalmed - and hard to get apart.

For the next forty minutes there was a noise like an avant-garde drum solo as, resistant to the last, the wheelhouse was dismembered. Owen managed pretty well considering his disablement, fielding the pieces on his plaster-covered forearm as they came apart. These, then, could be stacked on the aft cabin roof. But, without this protection now, we suddenly felt exposed. It had not been part of the plan.

Bridges in the Netherlands are mostly of the lifting type. A barge can spend a lifetime there without the wheelhouse ever coming down. Hence the situation on *Secunda*, which throughout her long career had never, before I bought her, been beyond the country's borders.

France, on the other hand, is a land of mixed clearances. Thinking this to be the only such obstacle, and with rain on its way, we put the wheelhouse up again. Then round the corner, of course, lay another. It was not just weight-training that the wheelhouse provided, it was a test of self-control.

Happily, on the bigger, busier waterways towards the Seine, the bridges were high once again. Giant barges thrashed by, laden with grain, fuel-oil or fertiliser with, in their wheelhouses, aspidistra plants and lace curtains; the bric-a-brac of family life. Encouraged, we put our own up again too, to fill it with accounts books, paint pots and the wreckage of lunch.

The waterways of northern France are not all dreary. The Canal de St Quentin, in particular, for much of its length passes through attractive rolling countryside. The Canal du Nord, however, is the quicker route, a broader, deeper waterway, running farther west. Less varied and for the most part straight, this was the course that we took. The Nord's modernity somehow builds up melancholy, for its concrete-lined expanses sit uncomfortably in the rain. Begun early in the twentieth Century, its construction, overwhelmed in each of the World Wars, was only completed in 1965.

My father fought at the Somme and often, as we made our way southward under grey skies, I would think of him. Once, when we moored for the night, a horse and cart plodded by in silhouette along the road nearby, a spread of furrowed fields beyond. It could have been 1914 again.

The River Oise, wide and muscular, sweeps away such introspection. Here the barges were pounding along in a devil-take-the-hindmost parade, packing into the locks in a display of pent-up vigour that in England would be beyond belief. The Seine, which follows, is likewise busy; a waterway on which, if you hit trouble (and Harry's belts, despite much attention, were slipping once again) there is the anxious feeling that all anyone might want is for you to get out of their way.

Paris, sparkling in early summer, afforded a pit-stop. The Impressionists were on show in the Jeu de Paume, beside the Tuileries garden. As in most art galleries, it was best to visit in the morning, before too many other visitors got in the way. Here, magically captured, was much of the allure of the country. The moorings Monet painted at Argenteuil had been there for us too as we entered the city, the water dancing in the sunlight. Travelling afterwards out of Paris to the suburbs beyond, towards the forest of Fontainebleau, the thought of these paintings returned time and again as France unrolled.

At Melun a prison has been erected by the water's edge, with towering walls, beyond which, from the vessels passing by, the windows of the cells can be seen. At one of these, plaintively, and for a very long time, someone was waving to us.

By now the wheelhouse was once more an integral part of the boat. Porch, conservatory and living room, this was our command post. All the more then the shock on entering the Canal du Loing, the first of the older navigations towards the centre of France, to discover it would have to be taken down again.

After a narrow escape near Nemours, following which Frank, who was generally abstemious, downed an early Cinzano Bianco, the wheelhouse was kept folded away, at least while we were travelling. That concrete, after all, had been an expensive waste of time.

Marseilles-lès-Aubigny, across the upper Loire from Nevers, was where we were aiming for now. There we would be establishing our HQ, our nerve centre. It was due to be our nervous centre as well, but that had still to come.

The Loire here is not that part of the fabled river with chateaux beside it. Those lie more towards the sea. Nor, as mentioned earlier, is this a region of widespread scenic grandeur. The canal, built alongside as a more reliable means of navigation than the quirky river itself, runs in straight-line jags. But its beginning is certainly picturesque, for at Briare a splendid aqueduct, with embellishments by Eiffel, takes the voyager across the Loire itself. A day's run farther south lay our destination, chosen after my meeting a few months earlier with our saviour, John Riddel.

In every business there must be flukes. This one came about by bumping into John at, of all places, the Boat Show in London. There John, who was Australian, was trying to drum up business on behalf of the cash-strapped hire-boat company down towards Nevers for which he found himself working. We, on the other hand, were looking for a base, or at any rate a mooring, somewhere in central France. We also needed a welcome - which, after an unpleasant dialogue with the waterway authorities in Paris, looked unlikely in that city. The hostility of two bureaucrats, sitting with their backs to the river in an office beside the Seine, certainly made an impact. Had we contacted them before work ever began we might well have given up entirely.

'Why not come to us instead?' John had ventured. 'The people are nicer there.' And so, after not much deliberation, the decision had been taken. Marseilles-lès-Aubigny it was to be, so central in the map that France, if hoisted in the air, would balance on it precisely.

It was at Marseilles-lès-Aubigny that we now found John himself. With him were Chris, the owner of the *Pisgah*, Chris's wife Vanessa, his dad and various others, only a few of whom seemed to be French, testing the products of Pouilly-sur-Loire.

Our reception, though affable, and meriting a few further bottles, did not stir this group to excess. A band, surely, should have been playing; but at Marseilles-lès-Aubigny, it turned out, arrivals such as ours took place on a regular basis. This, as Chris would explain, was the essence of the place. It was the way Marseilles-lès-Aubigny worked. We might as well get the wheelhouse up again, he said, for this was a spot where you waited.

Passing along the canal amongst the freight barges was that steady flow of other craft, yachts mostly, frequently British, and, by the time they got to Marseilles-lès-Aubigny, usually in trouble. Lured by the Mediterranean and unsuited to the journey in between, these visiting vessels, squeezing into the bank whenever they met something larger, could be quite knocked about.

Waiting as we were for John to shepherd us through the processes of importation and licensing, we would get involved in these crises. Brmm, brmm. It would be another boat approaching. There would be a red ensign, occasionally a blue one from one of those clubs entitled to fly them - although amongst the lock-keepers such nuances could be wasted; I was once asked, in all seriousness, after lengthy scrutiny of the 'Red Duster' we were so proudly displaying, whether or not we came from Russia. There would be voices too: 'I say. Seems to be a boat base. Perhaps we can lie against that barge,' etc.

And so they would stop, with their sagas of burned-out alternators, their bent propeller shafts and the fact that, after so many delays, Mollie had to get back to Chislehurst to clear up the sale of their house. More often than not *Secunda* would have such a vessel alongside, while parts were sent for from England and people borrowed our tools. Frequently, through a process of osmosis, they joined the Marseilles-lès-Aubigny workforce.

Chris and Vanessa from the *Pisgah*, it transpired, were allowed a free mooring provided they cut the grass. Hugh and Noel, stranded in a lifeboat, could have their engine restored in exchange for renewing the many panes of glass in a semi-derelict shed. Mabel and Mark, who should have been in Corsica long before, were cleaning out the hire boats. Quite what our own role would be was not yet clear, though there were rumours of *Secunda* being used for a reception of some kind, for officials John had it in mind to cultivate.

The boatyard itself belonged coincidentally to another neighbour of Luke's, who, attracted by the gaggle of hire boats an Englishman named Jim had collected, had bought the business up. Guardedly now, bringing to bear all his farming expertise, he was attempting the very difficult feat of making the place pay for itself.

Hence the bartering. Jim hated the paperwork, anyway, while John was no great mechanic. So the two of them changed places, to be joined by Charles from Germany, who was a really good mechanic and who was likewise passing through. Jim, by the time we came along, was leaving to take up goat-farming.

Though different architecturally, and without the smell of sea air, Marseilles-lès-Aubigny, as Portia was to remark when she came out to join me, shared several similarities with Brownsworth.

In theory, by now we should have had the *Secunda* assessed for import duty by the customs people at Bourges, then approved by the canal authority and given a licence. But we were unusual, and unusual things were avoided in France, at least in this part of France. They attracted the word 'No' from the *fonctionnaires*. It did not mean 'No', necessarily; more often 'Why don't you just clear off?'

Vessels such as ours were rare in this neck of the woods. Richard Parson's dealings had all been in other parts of France. In any event, negotiations with authority, which Richard abhorred, were masterminded not by him, but his colleague Guy, who, being French, knew how things ran. At Marseilles-lès-Aubigny, on the other hand, and for a considerable distance around, there were no clear precedents. 'Paris?' said Monsieur Frouin of the Navigation Office at Nevers when we mentioned our difficulties earlier. 'What's Paris got to do with it?' Provincial France, we were discovering, looked for no clear guidance there. Nor, it became apparent, did one département take much notice of another. Amongst such islands of independence it was important to have chosen the right one.

Chris and Vanessa's ship, the *Pisgah*, having arrived a few weeks earlier, had her nose ahead by a margin, to the extent that a customs man had actually come to look at her - giving sufficient notice, fortunately, for Chris to strew the interior with wood shavings as a means of downgrading her value. After this display, however, a slumbering silence reigned.

The département of Cher, in which Marseilles-lès-Aubigny sits, did not seem a region in which Archimedes might have rushed naked down the street shouting about his discovery. He would have been asked to go back and write it all down, with queries as to the spelling of Principle, before it could be filed somewhere, then hopefully forgotten.

Marseilles-lès-Aubigny, once upon a time, was a celebrated junction, a fulcrum of the waterways. There the ancient Canal de Berry, coming in from an area of far-flung spookiness to the west, met, in the big town basin, the canal that runs alongside the river Loire. In later years, the Berry canal would fade, falling into disrepair. The nearest thing to the narrow canals of England, with long, thin boats and on-going problems of water supply, it closed by official decree in 1954. Marseilles-lès-Aubigny, ever since, had been a museum piece, with ancient docks, the occasional freight barge passing through on the surviving main line, and one of those bars in which everyone stops talking as soon as you open the door.

In the waterway world a mystical aura can be assumed by places the average citizen will never even have heard of. In England there are several such: Great Haywood, a major junction in Staffordshire, Bull's Bridge in west London, Norbury on the Shropshire Union, where once a canal to Shrewsbury branched off. Marseilles-lès-Aubigny is the same. It is not Nevers the barge people speak of, the city a few kilometres away, but Marseilles-lès-Aubigny, named in irony after the great Mediterranean port.

Overshadowed in later life by the chimney of the cement works in the neighbouring village of Beffes, Marseilles-lès-Aubigny is appreciated best as a hangover from the days when the canals were slow-going areas of toil. Postcards showing barges hauled by mules fetch a high price now, but the atmosphere that they catch, with numb grey skies and people in overalls several stages short of haste, is rarely far away, even today.

A feature of our quay was the railway siding alongside and the creakings and groanings of the freight trains that mustered there. Once one of these arrived, which it did with extreme stealth, it would wait, sighing, seemingly for days, while the numerous personnel meandered about, bearing chitties from the cement works and noting the numbers on the wagons.

That they did this slowly could be accounted for by the bar behind one of the boatyard sheds. There, in their zeal, John and his colleagues had established licensed premises, the bar itself constructed from the sawn-off portion of a *Berrichon*, one of the ancient mule-drawn vessels from the moribund canal. Varnished, with its cast-iron bollards still in place, the bar was a splendid creation, the delight, so it was hoped, of those who booked the hire boats.

In the event, the customers rarely went there, being anxious to be off on their holiday cruises or, if returned, on the way back home. By way of replacement there came the railway workers, whose tour of duty actually began at the bar, fortifying themselves for the long day's pottering amongst the wagons, with a return each hour for what they called a *canon*, a glass of *vin ordinaire*, at the government-regulated price.

Even with the jobs-in-exchange-for-moorings programme, the bar staff to meet these long and peculiar hours could not be provided. So the place closed down, leaving the railway workers to wander into the village instead.

With the sidings on one side, and some broken-down British yacht on the other, *L'Esprit de Brownsworth*, was in danger of catching up with us again. Madness loomed. What was needed, and quickly, was a trip of some kind. Any kind.

No tax collector, no representative of the Bourges Chamber of Commerce, however much they should, officially, take notice of us, looked likely to be doing so in the next few days. The Canal du Nivernais beckoned, the gloryland I once inspected in the *Arthur*, our stamping ground to come. Scenic, and at times dramatic, this is the ultimate backwoods canal, climbing into the hills from its own connection with the Loire, then descending to Auxerre in the north. An early trip there might help in relieving the pressure.

The southern entrance to the Nivernais lay just a day's run farther south. With Portia and I came Charles, the first of the crew members employed back in England. His qualifications, a degree in French and an enthusiasm for narrow boating, looked right at the time. Indeed, he was to prove an agreeable and contributory colleague, disconcerting though it was to discover the Cambridge notion of French was not the everyday variety, but inclined towards Proust and the journals of Baudelaire. When, a few weeks later, Charles got into confrontation with the legendary lock-keeper at Crain, the farther side of Clamecy, who harboured a persecution complex over people sampling her pears from an overhanging tree, it was as if a fellow of an esteemed scholastic order was meeting one of the Flintstones.

Alas, and with a curse upon the Chief Engineer at Nevers, with whom I had laboriously corresponded, the Canal du Nivernais in no way lived up to the depth of the navigable channel that gentleman had indicated. As happens in England also, a self-protective amnesia had descended. Practical evidence notwithstanding, the canal stayed as deep, in officialdom's mind, as it had been thirty years before.

That the countryside was blissful was both consoling and a frustration. There was a fortified farm, with turrets. Geese hissed in unison. Following this was a lock-house, in which the cast-list from a tale by H E Bates came tumbling out, cackling with joy as they whirled up the sluices, before returning indoors for further bacchanalia. What were they on? The huge-bosomed lady, grinning from ear to ear as we made to depart, leaned across and said, in effect, 'What rattles your cage? Have a good time folks. We certainly do!' They, for sure, had no worries about customs duty, or the managers of banks. Or if they had they would have seduced the bureaucrats concerned, laying them flat with the local *grappa*.

A sublime section followed. Predatory birds wheeled above the meadows. Then came a lift-bridge, with a chateau beyond.

Thoroughbred horses grazed. There was wood sedge, with water voles and bright blue butterflies. Walt Disney would have loved it. But, with *Secunda*'s gearbox glowing from the effort, we concentrated instead on our passage past various blades of grass. In the canal was too much mud. And, in *Secunda*, alas, too much concrete. We were going very slowly indeed.

'Salonga?' said a keeper, while *Secunda*, at the pace of the hand on his company watch, edged her way into the lock. He looked at us quizzically as, in a pattern that was common, his wife abandoned the housekeeping to come and wind the sluices. He was amiable enough, all the same, if hard to understand. Even Charles could not make out his purpose.

'Salonga?' He said it again as we wrestled with a creaking gate. On the Nivernais the equipment matched in obtuseness those who were put there to manage it. Then he turned to me. '*Anglais*?' he enquired. '*Vous-êtes Anglais*?' Then came the punch-line. Looking solemnly down the towpath, he began to sing. 'Salonga way to Tipperary, salonga way to go …' He had been an infantryman at Amiens in 1918, with a wound on the knee to show for it, exhibited like some relic, by hiking up his trouser leg.

We were to meet him again twenty-four hours later, when, because we had given up and turned the boat around, we were able to repeat this conversation in all but the smaller details. He was a nice man, nonetheless, an ambassador, in many ways, for a waterway lost in time. It was a pity all the more that we could not get farther up it.

Returning onto the Canal Latéral à la Loire was like going to sea by comparison, and in the first of its locks there, we nearly hit the gates at the other end, so brisk was our progress now.

The lessons of this Nivernais trip were valuable, if worrying. Primarily, the prize route, the one we were billed to explore, was useless, at least in its southern part. Barge travel might be accepted as slow, but no-one wants it like that.

There was always the *northern* Canal du Nivernais, of course, on the other side of the hills. This, we knew, had greater depth. *Palinurus* went up it from time to time, and she was at least as deep as *Secunda.* There was even a bit of freight over there, barge-loads of grain mostly, to Germany and the Low Countries. The trouble with the northern Nivernais was the time it would take to get to it: back to the Seine, then the long haul up its tributary, the Yonne. It was a journey two thirds of the way round a circuit.

Meanwhile we had our first two passengers to carry, who particularly wanted to be in the region near Nevers. These were an elderly couple from Arizona, who, as it proved, negotiated all the hurdles our agent in England put before them, and still decided to come. Two passengers hardly constitute a quorum, but Françoise, the secretary at the boat base, volunteered to join us, while a freelance photo-journalist that I remembered and contacted by phone from a post office on the Nivernais, accepted my invitation too.

That *Secunda* was still neither imported nor licensed no longer seemed so important. These were *affaires en cours* which, in France, meant they could grind on *ad infinitum,* while we carried on as before. A more urgent problem meanwhile was to find some means of bringing our clients from Paris, then from time to time take them off in order to look at the sights.

Here was another facet of the business not taken seriously at those meetings round the stove. People coming on my earlier barge the *Arthur*, after all, made their own way out by train. Then from the station they walked. Nor did they expect to be shown much once they arrived. As waterway enthusiasts like ourselves, they regarded the canal as sufficient a spectacle on its own. But the passengers on *Secunda*, it was slowly beginning to dawn, would not be canal buffs at all.

Chris, of the *Pisgah,* faced the matter practically, hunting down a Ford Transit van to carry his passengers about. Previously used in the tobacco trade in Birmingham, it came to him cheaply, the previous owners, after a foray into smuggling, having now gone to prison. With some second-hand seats installed it became the kind of vehicle in which jazz bands went to gigs; but at least it was a bus of sorts.

For us no such bargains were to be found, although a hastily struck deal yielded my brother's Ford Cortina. With just two Americans to think of - and very few to follow - that would have to do. The journalist and her husband, when they arrived, would do so in their own car, and this, hopefully, could be added to our fleet for the week.

That the cruise went well enough was due largely to the two who actually paid. The input Americans are prepared to make I have come to appreciate greatly. They want the event to be a success, and thereby help to make it so. The catering was done by Pippa, a friend of Portia, whose real job was with the BBC. And she was great, cooking in the French-influenced style that in Britain was just catching on.

With the week well under way, the journalist and her husband staged a cameo drama by waiting a couple of hours at what they failed to perceive was the wrong bridge, on a derelict arm of the canal so covered in duckweed it might have been walked across, and which, plainly, had not seen a vessel in a generation.

That they had omitted to heed instructions on their ramble could not be sensibly discussed. The Customer Was Always Right - and not just that, the Captain was expected to grovel. I would not have minded had they actually paid. Our Americans, on the other hand, remained positive throughout.

I am horrified to think now of what we offered: the poky beds, the lavatories down a corridor, the lack of ice (Harry S's contrivance having packed up yet again), the to-ing and fro-ing in a beat-up motor car.

Albert and Marion Ramond, from Phoenix, Arizona, professed to have enjoyed that first cruise, and maybe in some respects they did; but they were also understanding and kind. These many years on, I am still deeply grateful.

That cruise was a shake-down, concentrating minds. At least, it concentrated mine. Those trips in the *Arthur* had been seriously misleading. Travelling with friends then, the spirit had been one of exploration. With *Secunda*, on the other hand, our clients expected us to be organised, and, to know the region already.

Pondering this, with a vow to at least read the guide-books, I concentrated meanwhile on sorting out the storage for laundry and the bewildering array of supplies that even a handful of passengers appeared to need.

It did not do, we had found, to put any of these things under the seats in the saloon, for getting them out again messed around such clients as might be sitting there. Nor was the area beneath its floor much better. There was space there it was true - reminiscent of the set for a mining disaster movie - but reaching the entrance required a journey across the saloon first of all, with every possibility of entrapment in passenger reminiscence. As many things as possible, we came to realise now, should be kept out of our client's orbit altogether. We would put them in our own quarters instead.

One of *Secunda*'s plus points was the area accorded to the crew. Later, when I became familiar with other barges, I was to realise how spacious ours was. On *Palinurus* three people packed into the bow, one lived in an over-sized orange-box down in the bowels of the ship, while the Captain and his girl-friend occupied a rustic steel hut on the after deck.

There is often discussion amongst the passengers as to who in the crew might be sleeping with whom but, as a general rule, even in this liberated age, those on a barge prefer to have a separate cabin each and to conduct such liaisons as might occur to them with discretion.

Up in the bow, I shared the cabin there with Portia, discovering at an early stage that some insulation beneath the dark steel deck would have been a good idea. Going to bed otherwise at any time before 2 am, in the heatwave experienced that year, was akin to climbing into a cooker.

That we were perilously short of money by this stage influenced practically everything that was done. Shelving, when it was required, was constructed from old plywood offcuts. Harry S's belts, rather than being hurled onto the dump, continued to be wrestled with daily, in a vain attempt at getting ice; for a refrigerator - and it would have been a special one, running off a low-voltage supply - was at present out of the question. We in the crew lived frugally, while at night-times I stayed up and worried.

4: EARLY DAYS

A diversion arose, as unexpected as it was time-consuming. It concerned a photo I had taken, several years before on the *Arthur* trip. And the lock-keepers now, on discovering this, decided that they all wanted copies. In the interest of user relations, for John Riddel's organisation at least, this now became important.

The picture itself was of mules pulling a barge on the Loire near Decize - one of the few points at which the canal alongside gives access to the river itself. Such procedures had persisted there, a hangover from the days before the Second World War when 80% of the barges in France were moved around without having motors themselves.

By the time the *Arthur* arrived, mule haulage had in principle been banned, a consequence of its tedium and the delays that it brought. For the speed the mules moved at, so slow the tortoises of the Galapagos would have stood an even chance, caused those who had motor barges, whenever they overtook them, or tried to - which is difficult when there are locks in the way - to gnash their teeth and weep.

Decize, however, was an exception. Shaded by poplars, a lightly-used branch linked the canal beside the Loire with the big, wide river itself. There, at the joining point, the mules, long-eared reminders of practices otherwise gone, tweaked barges loaded with sand out of the current and into the adjacent lock.

That they could achieve this, in a sandbar/circular eddy situation so complex it would take a Master's thesis to describe it, depended on the magic moments at which their driver, René Guichard, tapped on the towline with his stick. If he did this in a certain way, the mules started. When he did it again, they stopped.

It was the tapping that made the difference. René had been brilliant at it, top man in the field, and when he died, that aspect of the business died too. For no-one else could manage this task at all. A tractor had to be used instead, and the barges got battered about.

Meanwhile my photo, greatly enlarged at the behest of John Riddel, adorned the short-lived Marseilles-lès-Aubigny boatyard bar. There, in theory, the picture might have stayed; had not one of the lock-keepers called by, lured by a glass of Sauvignon at 80 cents the thimbleful. From then on, the news travelled fast.

'Kick one and they all limp' they say in my home town in Cheshire, referring to the degree of interconnection in an old-time mill community. It can often be the same on canals. An extensive stretch of the Canal Latéral à la Loire, it now became apparent, was run by the relatives of René. And all of them wanted the photo. Marseilles-lès-Aubigny, in its miasmic fashion, was influencing our lives yet again. Could I provide those pictures, please, to keep this lot on our side?

Small matter to these good folk that *Secunda* and the company behind her might be so short of customers as to be tottering, that the Captain would increasingly be waking in the night to do cash-flows - real ones, not bits of make-believe - so horrendous that he fell back babbling. The lock-keepers did not have our concerns. What about those photos?

The telephone, when I could get to one, which could take a chunk of the day, rang with instructions to Marion, Bob's secretary in the insurance office, upon whom the company papers had been dumped. Could she look in the third drawer down on the left, see if the negatives were there, then get them printed?

'Look, John,' came the reply, 'we've just had a letter from those people who made you the windows. They're getting their solicitors in …' *Merde* again. I thought we had paid them. Not paying our bills: embarrassment was hardly the word.

'Frame 34 I think it will be. Or maybe it's 34A. The one with the old chap and two mules. No, mules, not meals. Big things! Got four legs …' The line had gone crackly again. 'We need at least ten prints.'

'Luke's been on, as well,' Marion would persist. 'Says he's worried about the way things are going. Wants to call you back for a meeting.'

'If you could do another couple for Uncle André ….,' the lock-keeper at Abron said shortly afterwards. Had I a pumpkin handy I would have crowned him with it.

On top of these requests came the long-expected inspection of the vessel. This critical visit, we learned, would be conducted by Monsieur Bertrand, the supervising engineer of the Marseilles-lès-Aubigny patch. With him would be The Chief from Nevers who, as the non-authority on navigable depths, had lured us into the Nivernais in the first place. Coming also would be A N Other, variously predicted along the quay to be a fire officer, a man from Health and Safety, or some other trouble-maker.

As well as ourselves, *Pisgah* would be looked at also, together with a hire boat in John's fleet which some investor had been persuaded to sponsor. With this encounter coming up it was harder still to get to sleep at night. Out here, despite the food, the wine and the camaraderie, there always seemed something to worry about. It was apparently the nature of the trade.

Monsieur Bertrand's was a name on many lips. 'He's legendary,' Chris Ryle said; but I had not yet met him. As Engineer in charge of many kilometres of canal, Bertrand the Legend had plenty to think about. Nor did his responsibilities stop there: the mighty Loire was part of his empire as well. While navigationally this wide, willful river had been dead for a century and a half, the government, with a rush of blood to the head, was putting a nuclear power station beside it.

The accompanying dams, intakes and bridge reconstructions that this entailed made it remarkable Monsieur Bertrand should come to our neck of the woods at all. Sensibly enough, he had his office down at Sancerre, where the background was of wine-making rather than freight trains.

An incident with *Pisgah*, however, compelled a visit from him beforehand, in furious bad temper by the sound of it, at what, without doubt, was a serious waste of his time. This we had missed, being stuck on the Nivernais when it happened, on our abortive trip up there. By all accounts we were lucky that was so. Understandably miffed at the distraction from his nuclear concerns, Monsieur Bertrand, it was reported, resembled an intergalactic missile going off.

What had happened was that the *Pisgah*, after entering the dry-dock for repairs, proved unable to get out again once these were over. The dock was a shallow one, and *Pisgah*, having bounced her way in through some forceful driving by Chris, was wedged on the bottom.

In the end, after lots of revving and shouting, and Charles the boatyard engineer giving instructions in the no-holds-barred fashion that he had, the keeper of the locks just above was approached and persuaded to open his sluices. The level rose, *Pisgah* floated out and all would have been well - had not the extra water invaded the downstream village of Beffes. The keeper there, an old woman in every respect but gender, found that the canal, having lapped above the kerb, was pouring into his cellar. The arrival of a loaded freight *péniche*, making her way, as such vessels do, with a wall of water ahead, sent a further surge across the path. This flooded the poultry enclosure as well.

The Marseilles-lès-Aubigny man was delighted by this for, as often on the canals, where feuds can persist with Sicilian longevity, he and his colleague downstream were not on speaking terms. But the furore went to higher authority, and Monsieur B had to join in. The colourful experience that this proved to be made us all the more nervous now he was visiting again.

The night before the visit, Chris and Vanessa shared out a bottle of Pouilly Fumé, but the more we tried to cheer one another up, the more did gloom set in. Should our vessels fail, we would be done for.

Monsieur Bertrand, when he arrived, did not look particularly legendary. He had a Julius Caesar haircut, that was true, but in stature he was average. In a silver-grey lightweight suit he had a measured affability that was encouraging. The furore over the *Pisgah* had plainly been put to one side.

The Chief from Nevers, older and nearing retirement, had the world-weary look of someone fighting a losing battle. The main route through his area, built on the sand of which the valley consists, was in the habit of collapsing and forever in need of shoring up. The Canal du Nivernais (South), I could see now, would rarely be on this man's radar.

The third member of the team proved to be the official from the freight bureau in the village, to which the crews of the freight barges went most mornings, to check their positions on the waiting list for cargoes and to fill in lots of forms.

The meeting, in the end, was a charade. I mean no disrespect in this. These men knew, no doubt, what was what; but, provided we presented them with nothing appalling, saw no need to make a fuss. They had other concerns, and, anyway, it was Friday. John, who had his own axe to grind in getting his hire cruiser accepted, managed to exhaust their attention over her details so that by the time they got to us it was largely for formality's sake, before it became decent to serve out a round of drinks.

For *Secunda* the file was produced, but no-one wanted to dwell on it now, and when John led them away for a gastronomic session at the nearby *Papillon Rose* - to which we all contributed and equally willingly agreed not to attend, lest our rustic French and general nervousness should damage the occasion - it became clear that our permits, after the lapse of time that adds endorsement in such situations, would be issued through the post.

Nowadays permits are not so easy to obtain. An abundance of rules within the European Community sees to that, and people are actually appointed to administer them, without the distractions of power stations or embankments that subside in the night. Rarely, and sadly, are they people with any practical experience themselves. Which is the better: some career *fonctionnaire*, whose previous job was organising the working patterns for people building a slip road, or a group of cagey geezers such as Bertrand, who looked you in the eye and used their common sense?

The next hurdle would be importation, the payment of duty upon coming into France. This stood at the time at 17.6% of *Secunda*'s value. It was the 'value' that was worrying. Could we get the Customs authority, the *Douane*, to accept a lesser one? Even then, could we afford the 17.6%?

The city of Bourges, the administrative centre for Cher, was taking on the status of Mordor, a centre of oppression and possible doom. Here sat the Chamber of Commerce, weaving its tangled web of edicts and requests for authorised translations. Here too, in a dismal industrial estate, lay the HQ of the *Douane*, who could see us out of existence.

But it was high summer now, that time in France in which offices drifted into a state of trance, with the majority of the people away on their holidays. Those left behind saw their role as little more than holding the fort. The time to be fearful in France is in early September, when the bosses of these places try to pep things up, herding their employees outside to be diligent at last.

Such a lull would be useful. And, indeed, a tentative visit John and I made to the *Douane* offices yielded the news that, though they knew about us, and would get us in their sights one day, their timetable, too, was presently in holiday mode.

As to the navigational part of the equation, it could likewise be ages before our new status, as a non-yacht, a *péniche-hotel* as they seemed to call *Secunda*, would be entered in the ledger. So we could continue, semi-officially, with *Secunda* as before, keeping quiet about such income as we received. It would hardly amount to a fortune, in any case.

Back in England Luke had persuaded some relatives to take a trip with us, while, in a stroke of fortune close at hand, John had a family from Chippenham whose hire boat had broken down so badly that our carrying them in *Secunda* would be bailing him out of a fix. We had payments to make to John otherwise, so the new arrangement would be useful. In the Marseilles-lès-Aubigny tradition, we struck up a deal.

Accordingly, then, with this mixed bag of passengers, ranging in age from eight through to eighty-five, we set off to the north, to circle back via the Seine, then its tributary the Yonne to Auxerre. Once there, the Canal du Nivernais, deeper at the northern end, might at last be entered.

We had a regular cook now, Penny Thompson, to be paid when we had passengers: at £45 a week, as I recall. Otherwise she received only her keep. It was a scandalously low rate when I reflect on her capabilities. Her food, which was excellent, continued in the French-influenced manner that Pippa had adopted. Decades later - she is married with two growing children - I thank her again for the determination she showed in the face of nil refrigeration, negligible cash, and the hatches overhead leaking when it was raining.

Penny arrived, I suppose, through the Old Chums Network - a system previously despised but increasingly now embraced. Even so, there could be hiccups. With the best of intentions the fellow-directors sent over a succession of oddballs to work as housekeepers or deckhands. As our cruising season lengthened and, by a series of miracles, passengers arrived from time to time, the sound of plates being dropped became familiar, as did mechanical mishaps and cock-ups with the ropes.

'Well, he seemed alright to us,' came an explanation later. 'We thought he might help you with that belt problem you had. He seemed to be good at taking bicycles to bits …'

'Did he ever put them together again?' I felt obliged to enquire.

Bicycles, gradually, were moving centre stage. Bikes are good with barges. They are useful for sorties to the bread shop - and for passengers, as it transpired, to trundle up the towpath in the spirit of youth rediscovered.

With the family from Chippenham chafing at the bit, we could grab some extra cycles from John. Funny little things that went on the hire-boats normally, their tiny wheels and hopeless gearing proved useful, as it turned out, in limiting the distances people might travel. Bikes? It was yet another of the things we had not thought through properly in those days back at Brownsworth.

The most glaring absence of all in the operation was a bus of our own. We depended on Chris who, when he had no passengers himself, would lend us his Transit. Then, from a mooring, I could drive our people off to visit the local sights. There was the occasional second-division chateau, furnished with whatever its owners could get hold of, and at one point a car museum, stocked at the time with an equally random selection, its vehicles with punctures and cobwebs on the steering wheels. The sooner we got round to the Nivernais, with its cathedral at Auxerre, the basilica of Vézelay and the vineyards of Chablis all within reach, the more of a show we might be making.

On the way to the Seine, however, lay the palace of Fontainebleau. This was a Grade One attraction and fortunately within range. Meriting three stars in the guide-book, the palace lay across the woods from the Canal du Loing. Our own visit there coincided with that of many children, whirling through the corridors in a fast-moving throng, from which might appear occasionally the arm or despairing face of one of the teachers supposed to be in charge of them. Into the Throne Room they poured, sweeping around Luke's aunties with scarcely a glance at where Louis the Fourteenth might have presided. Pictures shook on the walls. Tapestries quivered. These tiny people, to whom a trip to the Palace meant little more than the chance of a few ice-creams, were in prospect of shaking the place apart.

It took an attendant, a short, stocky man in the uniform of a bus conductor, to bring the throng to order. Rising from his chair in a corner, where he previously appeared to have been an exhibit, he sharply clapped his hands. There was a freeze-frame pause.

'Halt,' the attendant declared. He let the echo die. 'Listen. You are in a place of history. Here, in this palace, Napoleon took residence. In this room - in this very room! - is his throne. *Voila!* Take note.' There was a large, ornamental chair with an 'N' embroidered on it. 'The greatest man in France! Napoleon, he would not tolerate behaviour such as this. Walk quietly. Tread carefully. Show respect!'

He winked as he walked back past us, while, in silence, class and teachers shuffled away. We were pretty awestruck ourselves wondering whether, after years of duty there, the attendant had assumed, through association, the character of Napoleon himself. He was a small man, too, a living example of how force of personality conquers all.

Some of this spirit infected the lock-keepers on the Yonne as well. They too wore peaked hats and behaved, by and large, as if Napoleon had won. The Yonne is a majestic river, more so than the Seine, which it joins at Montereau. Avenues of trees line its banks. Sweeping grandly from the south, with a backdrop of hills across the cornfields and the occasional angler in a punt, it provides a vision to match the grandest paintings of France. But its locks, which come steadily on the way to Auxerre, are large and cumbersome, with a long walk round after opening a gate to get to the other side. As a result, we discovered, the keepers tended to be grumpy.

'Papers! No, these are not good enough! This looks like a *péniche-hotel* to me. A yacht? Pah! Oh, thank you very much, Sir'

It was gratifying what a bit of baksheesh could do, but the hostility could be tiresome.

'No, you cannot enter the lock. There is a freight barge coming the other way (*in half an hour's time; but since it takes a quarter of an hour to turn the lock round, then another quarter getting you through, I can't be bothered to do that*) And once the other barge is through, we are closing for the night anyway *(so go and moor in the brambles over there. Those ones, in the remote spot against the collapsed bit of bank with the sharp bits of concrete sticking out and nothing decent to tie to. And up yours, matey.)*'

The Yonne locks, the size of football pitches, often have sloping sides, built that way for strength, rather than convenience. Slimy and unwelcoming, these dreadful walls keep any normal mortal sufficiently far from dry land as to render gaining it a near impossibility. Only on our whizzing through the entrance, where briefly the sides are vertical, might crew members grip the railings like gibbons, to hoist themselves ashore - the whizzing itself being necessary because of the eddies with which these locks are too often blessed.

At Auxerre the route changes its name, to become the Nivernais Canal, its structures reasonable again, its keepers more humane. It was in the city itself, on the splendiferous waterfront, just below the Cathedral, that this early cruise, our second for which people actually paid, eventually came to an end. There would be a gap now. With time to spare after driving our party to Paris, I could go back to England myself, for a meeting.

Getting across the Channel in the 1970s was by no means as easy as it later became. The commonest and cheapest way was to head for the Gare du Nord in Paris. From there, at ten o'clock each evening, a so-called express trundled out to meet the ferry at Dunkerque. For those without reservations a single carriage was available, a very old one, standing in shabby comparison to the First Class accommodation farther back. Since the majority on board were out in the corridor, however, this did not matter much.

The ship, equally grim, deposited its passengers in Dover at an ungodly hour in the morning. Whence a further train, with the previous day's newspapers strewn about the floor, thought about it for an hour or so, then wandered off to London. There, by the time our meeting came round, I was not in a very good mood. We held it at a club in the City, to which one of our group belonged, a fusty place with leather armchairs and dried-up sandwiches served by haughty middle-aged men wearing off-white jackets. In an oak-panelled room the eight of us assembled to review the situation, then flail the air.

We were in a mess, it was agreed - one of the few things we were agreed upon - with few, pathetically few, customers on the books. Far from the 250 conjured up on cash-flows there were, for the rest of the season, just twenty-one of them, supplemented by 'cheapies', people we knew, coming along, almost as a favour, at a much reduced rate.

Going through the list of things that were wrong did not help the general *entente*. It was difficult to know where to start. The boat was too deep in the water, and, at any pace at all, absolute murder to steer. The concrete was a burden. Yet we had to get the wheelhouse down when we travelled anyway; so why have concrete at all?

Luke's electrician had left gaps around the wheelhouse floor, into which a rainstorm had all too willingly swept, to work its way into the engine-room. There, in a shower of flashes and bangs, much of the circuitry had blown. The WCs became blocked at the slightest provocation, with their pumps nigh-on unserviceable, having been installed behind panelling over which someone had glued, all too capably, many bathroom tiles. There was a device in the engine-room, meant to shut off the fuel supply in the event of fire, which went off of its own accord at Decize, stopping the engine dead. Had this happened five minutes later we would have been swept over the weir on the Loire there (no doubt solving many financial problems).

There was Harry's freezer to dwell upon, which had yet to produce a single cube of ice. A repair man had come to see us at Briare, after which hopes rose briefly when a film appeared on the tray inside. All on board gathered round to stare at it and it was agreed that, yes, it looked like the beginnings of ice. If not, it could certainly be considered as frost. Then the system collapsed again and that very small gain was gone.

On our cruise with the Ramonds we attempted to meet the problem by buying ice ashore. Butchers, we discovered, were a possible source. And so, for five francs each, from a surprised gentleman in La Charité, Charles bought a couple of frozen plastic pails. Then, when Mrs Ramond asked for a glass of Campari, I could excuse myself for a moment, tiptoe onto the side-deck and smash at the ice with a hammer. The memory of that jelly-shaped block sailing across the canal has lingered to this day.

The second bucketful, not to be lost so easily, was wrapped in a cloth before being battered. Then the shrapnel was put in a bowl; but, when tried, revealed a startling taste of pork.

The best place to get ice, it emerged, was the office of a camp site, preferably a municipal one, since these were larger and had more of it. At Auxerre one morning, before the campers wised up, we purchased the entire overnight supply.

Stories such as these did not improve the mood of the meeting, although there were a couple of positive outcomes. Firstly, Hector was prepared to take over finance, and actually seemed to relish the prospect of unravelling the mess with Pay-As-You-Earn taxation. Healthily, also, he took a less reverential attitude towards the French way of doing things. Britain now was in the European Community and, if barriers had yet to come down, certain stances, he felt, could be challenged. On the vexed matter of *Cartes de Sejour*, with which individuals from other countries, such as Britain, were officially approved, by the French, for work in France, and without which - according to certain people in France - they ought not to be there at all, he simply said 'This is contrary to the treaty of Rome. Ignore it.' Hector would be good for morale.

Equally importantly, Bob, having visited the hire-boat people who were hopefully handling our bookings, decided - correctly, as it turned out - he could make a better job of it himself. Already, in fact, he was building up contacts in the USA.

It was good to get the meeting over, and be back in France without being lynched. And the scenery now was wonderful. Having been rebuffed in our earlier attempt at entry from the south, by approaching from the north, we took the Canal du Nivernais by surprise, before whatever resistant powers it might possess conspired to prevent us again. Not only were we on it, we were moving. This was a magical route, little visited then, an amalgam of the best elements of waterway travel. From the expansive stretches south of Auxerre, where the Yonne continued to wind in and out, to the forested portions farther on, here was the stuff of dreams.

Immediately, too, Bob was finding more customers. They came at all sorts of prices, by all sorts of arrangements, through the agents he had set about contacting, and his willingness to assist with the questions their clients might be asking. There were gaps in the schedule, but amongst them bursts of activity. Passengers, by golly - we actually had two successive weeks when the boat was virtually full! Up there in the woods, and under the stars, citizens of New York melted into friendship with visitors from Northumberland, or Perth in Australia. Friendship, when you came to think of it, was what we provided most of all.

So the season moved on and, increasingly, the canal absorbed us. If, when newcomers came on board, they mentioned the international news, we tended to stare and look uncomprehending. The space-shuttle's flight passed un-noticed. Only the death of Elvis percolated through the network of lock-keepers and friends passing by (causing such a gloom at Marseilles-lès-Aubigny, we learned, that restoration of the boatyard shed there was halted for a day and a half).

'Back to the real world,' our passengers would say as, in Chris's boneshaker bus, they headed back to Paris. But ours was the real world, or so we liked to think.

There were incidents. The portion of bank on which a garrulous Canadian tipped back his chair during a barbecue at Châtel-Censoir proved to be not entirely land: on up-country waterways, moth-eaten along their edges, caution is always advised. We pulled the bits of bulrush out of his hair then stuck him beside the embers to dry. That he carried on talking as soon as he was retrieved was much to his credit. Those gatherings around a fire captured the spirit of childhood in many of those who came.

Later, with experience, we took to calling these halts 'bonfires'. The term 'barbecue' was far too grand. Already, in our brief career, we had learned a thing or two about these events. One was to have a proper meal waiting, for cooking on the bank was unreliable. Another was to be careful with the punch. With wine, as a rule, consumption could be monitored. With the aptly-named punch, supposedly a refreshing summer drink, the results could be lethal.

'Some lemonade, a drop of vodka, then a bit of lemon, do you think, Jane? Um … tastes a bit thin …Better put in more vodka. Oh, we seem to have run out. It'll have to be gin, then. Oh, do you think that's too much? A bit more lemonade, perhaps?'

On a warm, sunny evening, masked by misleading flavours, a dangerous amount could be consumed. In the very near future I would insist that a recipe be consulted - then followed.

'John,' said a figure who lurched towards me. He was from New England, a senior figure in the judiciary there, one of those Americans we had glimpsed on Richard's boats and hoped ourselves to become accustomed to, who spoke very slowly. They might not be thinking slowly, of course. More often than not they weren't. Behind the relaxed facade the mental cogwheels could be spinning. It was easy to be misled.

'John,' the figure repeated, blinking through the wood smoke. 'This is …' No quantity of dots can convey the slowness with which he spoke. 'This is …' he started to say again. There seemed to be a moon coming up, just a pale one, as it was still fairly light. And there was Venus. Or maybe it was Sirius. The night skies of Burgundy could be wondrous to behold. 'This is very ….' His summings-up in the courtroom must have been something. 'Very …,' he stated yet again. The pause that followed was so extremely long it seemed appropriate to prod the fire and rearrange the embers. It took even longer to realise that whatever it was that was 'very' would never now be defined. The fellow had stopped completely.

'We really should be careful with that punch,' Penny said afterwards, when the casualties were all in bed. 'Then they might still be awake by supper-time.'

It was becoming clearer by the day that the captain's role consisted of more than just guiding the barge. The steering would be taken for granted. Instead there came the questions. 'John, what's that crop growing over there?' or 'John, tell us about Charles De Gaulle.' The capacity to squeeze into a lock without whacking the entrance, to mend a water pump, or sort out the electric supply and unblock the plumbing, had to be matched by a preparedness to trace baggage lost by an airline, proficiency at First Aid, and knowing the times of church services. With these qualities it was useful also to have a grasp of politics, ancient and modern, agriculture with an emphasis on wine, architecture - and the standing of a baseball team in the USA itself.

Way up the canal we would meet Pierre, who would stand by the lockside with his paper. Pierre, once, had been in the Resistance. The paper, a letter from a United States general, was one of thanks for the help his group had provided in the years of the Second World War. What Pierre was after now was appreciation of this, as a means of getting a drink.

When several years earlier I came up here in the *Arthur*, I arranged for my mother, elderly and a widow, to join us for a week. With her eyesight failing, it was a last opportunity, perhaps, to recapture the spirit of those holidays of my childhood when, long before it became popular, Dad had taken us all, his family, onto the English canals for the very first time. From Auxerre we made our way to the watershed beside the hamlet of Baye, and the atmosphere of the canal, always vibrant, became more intense.

On that trip, as now, beside the final group of locks, Pierre came out to meet us, a shabby, unshaven individual with the valued bit of paper in his hand. It was difficult to believe him. Fighting the forces of Germany? In the back of beyond? It hardly seemed a theatre of war.

There were other canal people nearby, living in the cottages that stood, one beside each lock, on the last winding flight through the woods.

'What did Pierre do?' we asked the keeper up the line.

'Oh,' she said dismissively 'Nothing. Nothing at all'

Coming again in *Secunda*, these several years on, the responses were much the same. 'I wouldn't take any notice,' his present neighbour declared. 'He only brings that letter so you can offer him a drink.'

'There were lots of those letters,' another one added. 'The Americans gave them out. This is a quiet place. *Tranquil.*' And an arm was waved at the woods behind.

As to Pierre himself, he was reluctant to be questioned. 'Tough times,' he said, or something rather like it; but his speech was slurred. Likewise his wife, who appeared briefly in the doorway of their cottage, could not be drawn any further. 'People don't remember,' she added, then went inside again.

We gave Pierre a drink all the same, and wondered, vaguely, what really went on.

At the summit of the Canal du Nivernais lies a series of cuttings and tunnels, then beyond those a lake. The way through is narrow with a one-way system, managed at the time by a Mother Russia figure living at the top of the flight. Communicating by hand-cranked telephone with the browbeaten soul farther on, she would enjoin us to wait as if it were a battleship coming through. 'No! You must stay. There's a vessel in the cuttings already!' A tiny plywood cruiser would at last appear, its occupants quailing under the supervisory glare.

They were right to do so for amongst the lady's other functions she supervised the lock staff on the descent towards Auxerre, with their quaint working practices and eccentric interpretations of the lunch-break. 'Now,' she would declare. 'Off you go - and don't hang about! We had people in there, just a week ago, who stopped to gather blackberries!' As if we would dare.

It was worth the build-up. Branches brushed the boat on both sides. Waterfalls splashed down alongside. There are legends about these cuttings; that they were dug by prisoners under Napoleon, using their bare hands, that the pit that lies above, where vipers nest, marks the point where some earlier works once collapsed.

It was in this region that the building of this waterway began, as a means of floating timber to the rivers. The work took a long time, with stops and starts for the Revolution and the conflicts that followed. Of the tunnels here, two of them are short; then, at 760 metres, comes the Souterrain de Collancelle, high-arched, with a narrow path within. Shafts extending upward through the roof provide circles of daylight and, often, a curtain of water, tumbling after rain.

Beyond this tunnel and a final leafy cutting lies the lake of Baye, a glorious open expanse, separated from the channel by a wall to moor against, with views towards the setting sun. To drive from here to Paris, as I sometimes had to do, was the wrench of the week. To return there afterwards, was to call again at Paradise.

5: GETTING BY

The notion of marketing was beginning to filter through. It was sobering to compare Stanley's promotional efforts with our own. It was only a start, but at least now we could prepare a decent brochure, with pictures of the boat on the move.

The brochure with which we started had been a two-colour affair, that is to say in black ink on buff-coloured paper. It was the best we could afford and its production, by no means easy, took us into the flickering, half-lit world of a fellow called Manny.

Already, Dick Everitt, a colleague from my days with *Practical Boat Owner*, had drawn the *Secunda* to go on our letter-head for a fee of £5. That he did it in a single lunch-break says much for his expertise. Another friend, Tony, who was working his way through art college, undertook the brochure design in exchange for a holiday on the boat; and his work was excellent too. The problems came with Manny.

Since the boat was still being constructed at the stage when we approached him, there could be no convincing photos. Drawings would have to do instead. Manny, we were told, was a fine artist, the very person we needed. The trouble with Manny was that he never did anything on time. And lateness, for him, was not a matter of hours. It was months. The range of excuses was spectacular.

'Look here, Manny,' I found myself spluttering. 'We hoped to get this brochure out last September. Now it's February!'

'I know, I know,' Manny would mumble. 'Don't go on at me, John …' There would be a pause while he thought of what to say. Had he got ink in his eye again? Did he have the flu? It was time to hold your breath, fascinated as to what might follow. 'It's been a very tricky morning,' Manny continued. 'Joan's not speaking to me …' Another pause followed. 'You see, I nearly killed the cat.' A complicated saga involving the old urban folk-tale of shutting the beast in a washing machine then followed.

When the drawings came at last there was a lovely one of *Secunda*, based upon a photo of her in the unconverted state before the work began. There was a so-so one of Rabelesian characters drinking wine, another, for reasons unclear, of a kilo of leaks and a rotten one of a woman in a bikini, performing aerobics on deck.

As we learned later, Manny farmed out his work. A Fagin of the illustrative world, he ran a network of hacks who, by the nature of the set-up, became so confused by the messages passing down that anything might happen. Manny himself lived in a fantasy world, fishing excuses from a bottomless sack of his own creation. He should have been a scriptwriter.

Now, on the Nivernais, with September upon us, it was time to get the next brochure under way. If people noticed my absences from the dinner table it was because I was writing copy, scaling such photos as had been taken, then packaging them up for Tony. Talking to him directly involved a visit to the post office each time, since that was the only place with telephones; so instructions had to be prepared as well; but at least it was a Manny-free experience.

The majority of lock-keepers on the Nivernais were women, given to coming out in their aprons then dashing back in order to rescue supper. This enabled husbands, usually, to have another job elsewhere. With a house provided, together with the right to several fruit trees and a living wage as well, this enviable arrangement had just one serious flaw. It was the boats that caused the bother. Would you believe it, ours was the second to have come along in the past three days! How could anyone be expected to plan their shopping, or visit Uncle Stephane in Corbigny if these boats kept turning up?

Despite this line of thinking, the women of the locks here were a more amiable bunch than the brigade down the Yonne, whose notion of diplomacy tended towards spitting and reminding you of the time.

Perhaps it was a job that women were better at. For even on the Nivernais it seemed to be the male employees, or the masculine family members when it was the wife who was on the payroll, who caused the most fuss. With their tantrums over lunch break and our intrusion thereupon, or their reluctance to fix anything that was broken, they reinforced the notion that France, left to them, would deteriorate to the status of a Third World country.

When, towards the end of our season, *Secunda*'s propeller became hopelessly entangled in a sheet of reinforced rubber, misguidedly laid on the bottom of the canal to prevent it from leaking, it was a woman from the lock below who came to help. The sheet, thick and strong, the size of a tennis court, was frayed enough for us to pick up one of its skeins. Using a bread knife, then a saw, we managed to cut it loose sufficiently for a rope to be attached, in the hope of dragging it clear.

The supervisor for this part of the route, Sergeant of the Nivernais Light Infantry, Woodland Division, Prime Gatherers of Walnuts and Occasional Cutters of the Grass, was, of course, nowhere to be seen. It was Barbara, a newcomer to our crew, going up the towpath on a bicycle, who found the fellow. He was just a short distance away, in the official canal-side hut, gazing into space in a condition bordering on catalepsy. Goading him into action took a little time, though once the rope had broken and he had fallen into nettles he was no use anyway. The sheet was not his idea, he told us. He'd always said it was stupid, and it was time to go to lunch.

We got it off in the end, a performance which took a day and a quarter, while the woman from the lock said she would call into head office in Corbigny to tell them it wasn't good enough.

It is a measure of how undiscovered the canal was at the time that, throughout our being stuck, not a single boat was delayed, not one. In the event the obstruction stayed just a couple of weeks more, before the next big boat along, which happened to be *Palinurus*, tangled with the sheet again, rolling it up like a carpet.

Richard nowadays was going from strength to strength - and his fleet was expanding. While *Palinurus* continued to be busy, so too were the other craft he and his colleagues had acquired: the *Water Wanderer* on the Canal du Midi, and a sizable vessel on the Yonne north of Auxerre that, after a number of changes of name, came to be called *Escargot*.

Neither of these, it was gratifying to note, had the individual 'bathrooms' so widely promoted for Stanley's fleet. So there was hope still for us there. What their company did have, though, was the boost of a widely-read book. In 1967, shortly after Richard began, the writer Emily Kimbrough hired the *Palinurus* for a group of her own.

Attracting Emily Kimbrough was a hugely successful coup. Her books, which were travelogues really, written in a life-is-a-party kind of style, had a following in the USA. *Floating Island* was published soon afterwards and in it Richard, as Captain, emerged as the laid-back but able facilitator of a dreamlike voyage into bliss. Happily avoiding any reference to lavatories, *Floating Island* was pulling the customers in.

The days of communal WCs were numbered nonetheless. Stanley was responsible for that. And all the further craft that Richard and his colleagues came to introduce would have 'en-suite facilities', or 'bathrooms' as Americans liked to call them. For us to do the same, alas, without the money, was currently out of the question.

Throughout the season the numbers coming on board varied wildly, from full house to zero. When there were fourteen passengers, or even as few as six, they could to some degree entertain one another. Life became harder when there were only two of them.

Tempting though it was to cancel such a voyage, this could not be done. These people had made their bookings in good faith, with every prospect of other like-minded souls coming as well. They had arranged their flights accordingly, and places to stay at on the way. The contract had to be honoured.

When the numbers were low, we in the crew would join our guests at mealtimes. In such a situation lasting alliances can be formed; but when, on the other hand, the conversation returns, continually, to the traffic regulations of South Australia, it is hard not to nod. A week seems a long time then.

It was almost a relief after just such a session to drive over to Bourges again for the critical meeting with the customs officer there. Seeing him, the head *douanier* himself, as John and I had already done, was a privilege apparently. For what normally happened was that you dealt with a *transporteur*, an intermediary occupying, very often, the same building, whose business the customs insisted upon your using, on the basis that only the *transporteur* could understand the paperwork. The arrangement was a sophisticated equivalent of that to be found in India, where at the airport one person took your passport in order to hand it to another. The difference here was that they both charged money.

To short-circuit this process, even temporarily, had been unusual. Now, thanks to John's setting it up, we would be meeting once again the real thing, a customs man rather than the *transporteur*. This time, though, the crunch was coming: a price was going to be arrived at.

He was a shrewd-looking man of around fifty. His tie was sober, his suit sharply pressed. The eyes were penetrating. Furthermore, in fond recollection of an earlier career in the armed forces, his desk was adorned with model guided missiles. Nasty little things on plastic mounts, these were pointed at us.

At the earlier meeting the heart of our case had been the suggestion that craft such as *Secunda*, had little market value, being far too daunting for individual buyers to ever try and run. Chris Ryle, as we knew, had sold this notion regarding *Pisgah*, with just £600 to pay.

On the other hand, as the customs man pointed out, to assemble the *Secunda* as we had, undoubtedly cost a whole lot of money. He could impose the duty on his own assessment of that.

It was time to purse our lips, look shocked, then turn the conversation to rugby football - a widespread weakness here, and exploited by the group on the quay, without shame, whenever the going got tough.

He was not to be deflected. The discussion, picking up on our previous visit, moved now into delicate territory - the arrangement we had agreed to that, whatever valuation British customs put on the vessel, our man would now accept. It had not been difficult, of course, on the recent visit to England, to cook up a suitably low figure. 'Value £14,000' I had declared back at Brownsworth when Portia and I made a call. 'Just a formality. For the French,' I added, as if that justified everything. At which the customs man there, not having the slightest interest any more, raised his rubber stamp, winked, then pressed it down on the form.

It was far too low a sum. 'Not enough,' the *douanier* declared with an icy smile. Then he doubled the fee. A guided missile glare wrapped the matter up. 'I could charge you very much more if I decided to,' he said yet again. The duty he was asking for came to around £4,000. That finding this money could be difficult was not something to dwell upon in his company.

As a follow-up we moved to the *transporteur*'s office next door. There, through formulae of their own devising, they added several thousand francs for themselves, while arriving at a deadline to pay. With our season almost over now, we had done well to spin the matter out so long.

Now Chris's bus staged a small melodrama of its own. Messily, and without much hope of repair the clutch cable snapped. The vehicle was a Ford, and French people drive Fords occasionally, so in theory we could get the replacement part ... but in France the driver sits on the other side. This makes their cables shorter.

We were in the same position now as the Brits who rolled into Marseilles-lès-Aubigny - wondering whether to send back to the Old Country for bits and pieces, or limp on regardless.

With a little determination the bus could still be made to run, albeit in one gear only - the one in which we could push, then rush along after it in the hope of climbing on board. Since stopping meant stalling the engine, the crying need now was for a clear road ahead. 'Don't change,' came the unison shout as we rumbled towards the traffic lights at La Charité; but of course they did. Turning right there afterwards was a tricky manoeuvre, performed in the face of an oncoming tanker lorry and the baffled gaze of two gendarmes, posturing at the crossroads on their motor-bikes. With the starter motor churning and various gasping figures galloping up from behind, the scene was too complicated, possibly, for them to take any action.

Reaching Marseilles-lès-Aubigny in such a fashion summed up that first season. Chaotic is not quite the word, suggestive as it is of busy-ness throughout. In practice throughout the summer there had been gaps, some of them long ones, during which unease rose up in a cloud.

Those last October days, as the curtains were put away and the water-pumps drained, were as depressing as any. We were hardly finishing our season in triumph. Leaving the bus for the bits to be ordered, and *Secunda* by the railway line, we set off at last for England.

The farewells between us took place as the Cortina rolled into London. There, with a mixture of relief at our survival, and regrets at the parting of the bonds that had grown up between us, we split up.

In England there was another company meeting to arrange. It was held in the place with the kiln-dried sandwiches again, the club with the panelling and sobering boardroom table. The mood of the group, nonetheless, was more upbeat than expected. We were in one heck of a mess, of course, but there was hope in Bob's endeavours. Also, it was announced, the woman photo-journalist whom I'd invited, forgetting the failed rendezvous by the wrong bit of canal, had managed to get a piece published in the *Daily Mail*. So, there were enquiries coming in from that. Shafts of sunlight penetrated the clouds. It was time now to reflect on such operating blunders as we had made and to put matters right.

One of the lesser mistakes, but illustrative of our understanding, had been the charging for drinks on board. Wine served at meals was not included in this; but, in a penny-pinching exercise, we took extra money for liquor from the bar. Americans, in particular, did not like this. It looked petty and mean. Better to put up the overall price instead, we now realised, and gain ourselves some gratitude.

It had been three francs a shot for a Kir - white wine with Crème de Cassis - five for a Martini. Other drinks were similarly costed, including Marc, the brandy made from grape remnants. You could buy the bottles of this, for some reason, at a greengrocer's, or occasionally from a reeling group of gentlemen who toured the villages with a machine like Stephenson's Rocket that was actually a travelling still. 'John,' one of our guests roared back at me one day, as he staggered out on deck. 'I've just had a glass of that Marc. It was dreadful. It should be *minus* five francs on your list.'

A pad on the bar recorded these purchases, with a reckoning at the end of the trip.

'Mr and Mrs Elton,' I would say, looking upwards from my sums. 'Ten francs.' This was a little over two American dollars, or one pound and fifteen pence at the rate then prevailing.

'Mr and Mrs Sunbakker: eighty-four francs.'

'Miss Johnson ... three francs.'

'Father O'Flaherty,' I had to say on one occasion, '... six hundred and forty-seven francs.'

Despite these windfalls it was not worth going on. In terms of public relations it was all too embarrassing. There were, in any case, complex rules in France for selling drinks at a bar, involving, so the latest whispers said, application for a licence at every town that we passed. Liquor given away - even if it was not given away in the broader scheme of things - seemed to be exempt.

The import duty we had to pay nigh-on killed us off. Finding the money hung on my cashing in the pension I had contributed towards while in publishing. 'A foolish move,' I was advised when pulling the money out - though had it been left the company's rogue proprietor, the late Robert Maxwell, would have taken it for himself.

To this could be added such deposits for the year to come as Bob had managed to gather. I had my childhood stamp collection valued, but the difference it made was hardly worth the trouble. Thin Ice Enterprises, as privately we called ourselves, was on thinner ice still.

So short of cash were we now that even my own small wage could no longer be paid. To economise I moved back to join my mother at the family home in Cheshire, while Bob, who lived nearby, volunteered a corner of his office. With the cash garnered in tips from our passengers, and my mother's generosity, I might just get by.

Bob, by then, had taken over the bookings for good, the company empowered to do this having effectively given up. They were hire boat operators, after all, and, in that particular world, anyone with a half-decent set of boats gathered customers simply by signing with an agency, such as Blakes or Hoseasons, then letting them get on with it.

No, Mr Hoseason said when we approached him; he was not interested in hotel-barges. Those were a different kettle of fish, requiring more personal attention than an office such as his could provide. This was our problem: we were in a line of country where the people were a good deal more particular.

My mother, lonely since my father died, was happy to see me, pleased to have a role to fulfil. When the following season began, of course, I would be leaving, and she would be alone again, though the generation from which she came had a hardy view of emotional deprivation. Meanwhile, she cooked me stew, and fish on Friday, and did the laundry, and asked in a gentle way for stories of our time in France.

Hector came to see me, about British VAT, after which he sat down with us for supper and my mother liked that. I told her about the teapot that the Elephant Tea Company had produced in France, craftily shaped like an elephant, with the trunk as a spout, and how the tea dribbled down that spout, and how the lid, which was a special shape, could fall inside the teapot itself, and how we ourselves might take heart from its manufacturer's survival. But when I mentioned the visit I had made to Vichy with Chris Ryle and friends - as a break-out from the baleful effects of our mooring beside the railway line - my mother began to bridle.

We had found Vichy a fine-looking town, an echo, perhaps, of Bath, with fancy arcades and fountains around their walls. It was here that, after the German occupation, Marshall Henri Pétain set up his puppet government for the unoccupied part of France. A hero of the First World War, he was unprepared to endure a similar slaughter again. Unschooled in the details, it seemed to me a reasonable stance to have taken. 'Of course,' Mum said, with unexpected sharpness, 'people of my generation don't like to think of that place.'

Having until then only a shallow interest in France's role in the Second World War, I was finding my interest pricked. The appearances of Pierre by the lockside on the climb up to Baye were more and more intriguing. Nothing happened there during the Occupation, according to his neighbours. Was that really the case?

Chris Ryle, better versed than myself, filled in some of the gaps. The Vichy regime, totally collaborative, not only supported Nazi persecution but actively pursued it. The rounding up of Jews, and 'enemies of the state' was conducted with a determination even many Germans found surprising.

Vichy itself, headquarters of a supposedly puritanical regime, yet decadent, wrestles with its reputation today and would like to reinvent itself. But the reaction to its name prevents it. For many in France there has been, to use an inadequate word, an embarrassment about the Nazi occupation. It was scarcely surprising so few had a wish to discuss it.

My mother, from her trip on the *Arthur*, also recalled Pierre and the attitudes of his neighbours. 'People remember what they choose,' she said. 'It was a difficult time for France.'

The enquiries we were receiving via the *Daily Mail* article revived the earlier objective: of picking up customers in

Britain. Surely there were Brits who wanted to join us? And now, through the *Mail*, we could be getting some.

That there should be any difficulty in attracting British customers seemed extremely odd. Many of our nation's citizens were Francophiles, after all, while England, at least, had canal enthusiasts too. Surely they must want to come?

There were misunderstandings here that only dawned on us later. The canal enthusiasts, for starters, were keen to do it themselves. Not for them the passive role, while other folk ran the vessel. Even so, there was the remaining 99% of the population to work on.

Richard Parsons, however, provided a warning. Following a similar notion before we ourselves began, his company approached the BBC, who, after a bit of negotiation, arranged a feature with its TV travel programme. Joan Bakewell, something of a glamour figure in her day, came for a few days on board, to be taken to Vézelay, shown around a vineyard, and so on.

Programmes in this series appeared weekly at prime viewing time. Millions watched and, maybe because of this, reflecting the British attitude to holidays, they were money-obsessed. Cliff Michelmore, the anchor man, on describing a visit to Hong Kong, did little more than explain how cheaply he could get a suit made there. Price was almost everything.

Richard's business partners, largely selling to Americans, were naturally as keen as any to plumb the market in Britain as well. Sensing that fares would be the issue, they screwed up their courage and quoted the lowest figure that they dared. Given the small numbers the barge could carry, the size of the crew, the expense of running, the price was an absolute gift. It might have cost more than a package holiday in Majorca, but there was food and drink provided, collection from Paris and the visits ashore. In practical terms, for those who looked at the balance sheet, it was a loss-leader.

At the end of Ms Bakewell's spiel the figure was displayed in the middle of the screen: £125 per person for the week, posted up large, together with a contact address.

The results at first were gratifying. Four hundred responses were received, which, had they all come to fruition, on the basis of two paying passengers for each, would have filled *Palinurus* for fifty weeks.

It did not happen. Four people, just four, signed up. 'It cost us a fortune,' Richard said afterwards, 'in brochure printing, the time it takes to put the stuff in envelopes, then the postage.' Why didn't more come? 'In the end they decided it was too expensive,' he replied. Why then, had they enquired? 'Oh, lots of people do that after these programmes. They think for a while it might be fun, then they think about the cost. Americans don't look at it like that. They go for the experience, and they accept the price.'

This, now, we were beginning to detect in the *Mail* responses. We were receiving bookings, thanks in no small measure to the letters Bob was writing, but the fall-off rate was high. In the end - and it was not to be sneezed at, in fact a good deal better than the BBC did for *Palinurus* - we got 12 customers from that article.

This would be the picture for decades to come. The British, in particular, expected a holiday to be outwardly cheap. Willfully, almost, they forgot about the extras, the further money that came to be spent when they were out there.

Our Directorship pondered. The British market might be hard. But why not others? Why not - there was a hint of innovatory triumph as the suggestion was made - the Japanese? They were coming to Europe now (and being smaller, I privately concluded, were less likely to notice the size of the beds).

The idea was approved, and in my capacity, now that the crew had disbanded, of single full-time employee - albeit not recently paid - I was deputed to follow this up. Advertising in Japan was the first step. A look in the library located an agent who could arrange this. So I went down to London to see him.

He was a middle-aged man, and kind - kind enough not to take our money before, with an air of resignation, he told me what was what. He had an office in Dolphin Square, almost like a sitting-room, except for his desk and a Telex machine. Telex, the height of sophistication then, provided messages in a kind of telegraphese. The words were expensive and they were in capitals, but it was possible to get through quickly. Fax machines would not be appearing for another ten years; the Internet was unheard of. Most of our own communication was by letter. Using the telephone, particularly to the States, was costly enough to merit a serious discussion beforehand. We made such calls in emergencies only.

The agent sat me in an armchair, then poured out coffee. Though not an expert in tourism, as he explained, he did have some knowledge of Japan. Surely, he asked, these Japanese citizens, on what might be their first-ever visit to Europe, would want to see the clichés. 'As most of us do: the Tower of London, Buckingham Palace ...' or, if in France, 'the Eiffel Tower. After all,' he continued, 'if you were invited to Japan, would you, first of all, go on a Japanese canal?'

What a pity he was not on our Board. Had I been to Japan? 'No? The first thing I must tell you ...' He topped up the coffee. '... is that advertising in Japan is extremely expensive.'

'Well,' I responded with a bravery that was beginning to ebb, 'maybe it's worth it.'

'Very expensive indeed,' he continued. 'A simple small advertisement in the Central Tokyo Edition of the *Asahi Shimbun* - a daily paper, by the way, so people won't hang on to it for long - will cost around £600. It would, however, be looked at by over two million influential readers - assuming they opened the right page.'

'A picture of the boat,' I cried, recalling Dick Everitt's drawing for our letterhead. 'That will get them!'

'There is a technical problem there,' he went on, drawing a deep and obvious breath. 'Because of the way in which Japanese people read, the columns are laid out differently. The drawing would have to go sideways. Unless, that is, you spend much more.'

'We'll have a few words beside it,' I persisted.

'In Japanese.'

'No. It will have to be in English. None of our crew speak Japanese. We'll put it in English and those that can read it, well, those are the ones that we want ...'

'I have to tell you,' came the response, his patience beginning to creak, 'that to print anything in another language is extremely insulting in Japan. Anyway,' he added, by way of the *coup de grâce*, 'I don't think Japanese people particularly like French food. Too rich. And all those sauces ...'

So that was that. Another bum idea had been exposed, though fortunately, and unusually, before money came to be spent.

As a counterpoint to such defeats, a diversion was on offer: a busman's holiday, better still a bus-free holiday, on the waterways of old England. Archy had organised the very thing: a voyage down the Severn and the delivery of a narrow boat from somewhere in the Midlands all the way to Sharpness.

From his archives Archy found an old postcard on which to announce the idea. On the front of this was a *Titanic* memorial montage, reproductions from 1912, with a portrayal of the sinking ship, an angel and the words '*Nearer My God To Thee.*' On the reverse, dividing message and address was a silhouette of the luckless Captain Smith. From out of his beard Archy biro-ed in a balloon with the words 'It's a one-way trip.'

Portia was coming, and Bob, plus two or three others. It was boating in a group again, without the responsibility. There was the bonus, too, of getting within sight of the sea without having to go on it. I'd done enough of that in times gone by, thank you very much.

The Severn, robust and purposeful, has banks a little too high to see over. But from Gloucester southwards the course is by canal, the Gloucester & Sharpness which, in the whacky way of waterways, for many years basked under the title of Gloucester & Berkeley, despite not reaching Berkeley at all. It was a surprisingly soothing route, all the same, with temple-like housing for the keepers of the swing-bridges and views to the estuary alongside. Suitable also for our Barbarian purposes was the *Berkeley Hunt* at Purton, to get sozzled in.

The abiding memory of our trip, however, was of the heater on board. Robustly assembled from chromium-plated pipes, it stood in a central area. There, after a session with methylated spirits and matches, it could be persuaded to burn the diesel oil for which it was designed. It was an expensive item, apparently, which the proprietor of the boatyard, whom Archy had cajoled into letting us sail his vessel, was proud to make a selling point. Winter cruising, such as we were engaged upon ourselves, could now be undertaken in glowing good cheer.

Certainly the heater kept us entertained, for the hissing noise it emitted would change without warning to a menacing roar. A column of flame followed, licking up the pipework to threaten the cabin lining. At that point whoever was in the Talking Cupboard would come leaping out, trousers round ankles, to beat at it, crying for help in cutting off the fuel supply with oven-glove and pliers.

'You must have turned it up too soon,' the boatyard man declared when the time came to hand his vessel back. 'You have to let it warm up, you know.' Warm up? It was like dealing with a blowhole on Mount Etna. Perhaps he had made the thing himself. Only that could explain his attitude of denial.

All of which reinforced the policy we should have adopted for *Secunda* at the outset. Never try anything new yourself. In a world beset by dreamers, as boating certainly is, let others conduct their experiments for you. Remember also that many boats only get used for two or three weeks a year, so durability is hard to prove. For those in the barge business, where the season might run for thirty weeks, the flimsiness of yachting devices can cost the user dear.

Already in our brief commercial career we could furnish many examples: the flexible water tank which, because of the slight vibration, wore itself out at the corners; the patent malleable cloth with which, disastrously, we sealed the decks; the ice-making system, and so on.

At the Boat Show in London, the perpetrators of these devices might be hunted down. Even so, their resilience could be striking. The makers of the WCs, for example, having run the gamut of 'They shouldn't do that, Sir. Are they being used correctly?' came up with 'Ah, just a moment … Have you tried these, Sir?' Heavier valves, handed over free of charge, got me off their stand (although, when we tried them later, they made no difference at all). More often the stance was of jocular mockery: 'It's important to follow the instructions, you know,' followed by an armour-plated chuckle.

The problem with boating is that much of it is a dalliance. As Denny Dessoutter, the worldly-wise editor of *Practical Boat Owner* once confided 'Our readers are always getting ready.' Only a minority actually set out. So the equipment, by and large, rarely gets tested. Were it transferred to, say, aviation, the consequence would be disaster.

6: LOCAL LIFE

Where my mother lived, on the fringes of The Peak District, was once an industrial town. Then, with the demise of the mills, it became a sought-after region, with meadows to stroll in and the lure of the nearby moors. Towards Manchester, by contrast, lay surroundings a good deal tougher. The Wythenshawe Estate, on the boundary of the airport, was where Bob had his office.

'Sid Vicious is innocent' said the graffiti on its walls. Here, for economy's sake, Bob had started his insurance business. It was some way from the Burgundian idyll. The office block itself, promoted by the Council to generate a 'mixed economy', was beginning to fray at the edges. It was a good idea, when letters were posted, to make sure they caught the last collection lest, with what passed for wit in the area, someone set fire to them in the night.

Visitors during office hours came from a wider spectrum. A kaleidoscopic succession of characters called in: dealers in building materials, a succession of young men with uninsurable high-performance cars, the chip shop owner Mr Yin, who having filled in his form with no impediments declared, revealed, by way of polite conversation as he was leaving, that he was on his way to hospital to visit the boy he had knocked off his bike.

Then came Mr Lhadve, an Asian from Uganda, who would snatch up the telephone to conduct his own further business in native tongues, peppered with phrases in English such as 'Finest quality,' 'No credit' and 'Cash on the nail!'

'Aarh,' Mr Lhadve exclaimed one day, having slammed down the phone on someone in the immigrant community with whom he did not see eye to eye. 'These people! They're not like us - they're not businessmen like you and me, Bob!'

There was also Mrs Gordon. Mrs Gordon was the cleaning lady, a free spirit in the same grand tradition as the one at our first company meeting, who would talk to anybody, and very often did. Like some character in a far-out play, Mrs Gordon had the knack of the startling *non sequitur*: the price of lead, perhaps, or the amputation of her husband's leg. Dropped into the conversation, such topics could empty the most concentrated of minds.

'We're giving everything away now,' she said one evening while I was trying to draw up an advertisement for crew. 'Yes?' I replied, anxious not to seem rude. 'What?'

She bumbled around for a while, dabbing at the desks with a cloth, then pulled out a plug, regardless of its purpose, in order to attach the vacuum cleaner.

'What?' she said. 'Why …' She stiffened in the posture of the sorely-tried. Then she spelled it out. 'Malta,' she declared with emphasis. 'We give up everything here, don't we? First it was that car factory. The Morrison Minor one. Then it was Hornby Trains. That used to be British. Now we've given away Malta.'

'We've not had Malta for some time, Mrs Gordon,' I ventured. 'It's an independent country now.' I may have said 'I think it's an independent country,' so as not to appear such a know-all, but I need not have tried.

'No, no,' she said, tugging at the window-blind with sufficient force for Bob to call from the next room, asking if we were alright. 'Given it away,' Mrs Gordon continued.

'But …'

'Yes we have,' she stated firmly. 'It was on the Tee-Vee.'

There followed now, as often, a sweeping change of subject. 'What's it like being a Captain?' Mrs Gordon asked, knowing vaguely of *Secunda*, but very little more.

'Well, I'm not really a captain. It's just a barge on the inland …'

'It must be nice,' she interrupted. 'We went to the Isle of Man once.'

At which point Bob came to the rescue, to escort me off to the pub.

Reluctant as we were to face it, we needed a bus of our own. Chris, kind as he was, could not go on lending us his. Any fifteen-seater would do, provided that it ran; but these, in France, were impossible to hire, such were the rules there. So it was that we were drawn into the second-hand vehicle business, which could be perplexing. Gentlemen with oily fingernails spoke in cryptic terms of 'D-Redge Utilities' and our need for 'something like Terry's Bedford van'. They worked in barbed wire enclosures, these people, with Alsatian dogs for protection.

A succession of vehicles were inspected, making Chris's machine seem the height of sophistication. The noise of axle-bearings wearing thin became known to us. So did the fibs about careful owners and chances of a lifetime.

With our picky attitude, we were advised, the best bet was one of the auctions held from time to time in a neighbouring part of the city. There, we learned, handsome buses from the police force, or maybe the airport, were sometimes up for sale. It was a long shot, but surely worth a try.

At the auction house, a vast and echoing shed, a further facet of Manchester life was revealed. Through an arena like a circus ring, watched by men in sheepskin jackets, a succession of old wrecks was driven, engines roaring, while a fellow on a plinth, presumably the auctioneer, babbled his way through the Arabian Nights translated into Gaelic. Whoever might be buying, if anyone at all, was impossible to detect. Defeated, we crept away. There was still some time before the next season began and, anyway, the later we paid out our money the better.

First of all we had to get *Secunda* fettled up again. The crew could help do this. So, out to Marseilles-lès-Aubigny we went, crammed into the aged Cortina. Penny was prepared to cook again, thank goodness. The rest were new hands, unaware of many things, not least the nature of *Secunda*'s home port.

The flypaper effect of Marseilles-lès-Aubigny stayed as strong as ever. Over the winter several extra craft had settled in, their occupants already enrolled in the casual labour camp with which the hire boats ran. The railwaymen still circulated, fading away at weekends when a new set of visitors came to replace them, family groups from the village who would wander between the tracks then press their faces against the windows the better to look in (When French people are interested they make no bones about it: if you glare back they wave, then carry on staring).

Up in the village I was almost knocked off my bike by a Swiss-registered Rolls-Royce, which proved to belong to Stanley and Jarrett. It symbolised the differences between us. They were engaged on a tour of their less well-heeled competitors. Yes, the *Janine* was doing mightily well. Full in fact. So was her sister ship *Linquenda*. So, also, were the craft they were putting on the Thames, taking over to Belgium and thinking of buying in the Netherlands. I hoped our water-pumps would stop their banshee howl when our visitors stayed for lunch but, of course, they did not.

At least there would be ice now, from a second-hand refrigerator we were donated by a pal up the Nivernais. Running on bottled gas, it smoked heavily, which was why Ted wanted to be rid of it; but, with hands-on attention it could still be made to work. Why we did not buy one of these at the outset, instead of wasting our finance on the darker aspects of nautical fancy, I still could not consider without bashing my knuckles in a rage.

So many were their enquiries in the United States, Jarrett was telling us, they were actually turning them away. How many bookings did we have? Well, er, quite a few. And growing! We were always open for more, of course, all the same ...

Unexpectedly, the conversation brightened. Stanley, it emerged, since he could not build boats fast enough, was thinking of becoming an agent for other operators as well. If it was customers we wanted… Well, he said, as they made their way back towards a motor car costing more than the local chateau, he was prepared to think it over.

On that bonhomous note *Secunda* set off to Sancerre for a call on Monsieur Bertrand.

We were official now. The documents from the Navigation office had at last trickled through. With these came obligations. Whereas, in a 'yacht' we were permitted to waft around the system, threatening people with our inexperience, it was not the done thing in business. A *pilote*'s licence was required, with all manner of sanctions should we fail to have someone with one of these on board.

There were exams to be taken, forms to complete. With officials within the European Union beginning to discover the possibilities on canals for bureaucratic enforcement, such procedures looked unlikely to get any easier. The sooner the better, then.

Unjustly for that preoccupied gentleman, the person to see about this was Monsieur Bertrand. So far he had held me at bay, asking for one bit of paper or another. From out of the official *chapeau*, in the course of the winter, came the need for proof of my criminal record - or lack of one - for which, in France, there is documentation. A solicitor in Manchester solved that for me, with an oath upon the Bible. A dossier was also compiled of past boating exploits, together with papers about the company.

At his office in Sancerre, looking a mite less benign than before, indeed, muttering under his breath, Monsieur Bertrand applied himself to the matter. What, I wondered as I shuffled in front of his desk, would he be asking for now?

There are tests nowadays, wholeheartedly enforced, for those wishing to steer a barge, or even a motor cruiser (unless, mysteriously, she is a hire-boat, for which no licence is needed, thereby calling the bluff on the whole crazy thing). Text books are available, within which in diagrammatic form, ammonia tankers with engine failure drift sideways and out of control. Ferries set out, while tugs heave into view with loads of explosive in tow. There are cones, flags and boards, as people engage in regattas and other craft, previously un-noticed, begin to sink. Would any of this stuff be put to me now?

Alarmingly, Monsieur Bertrand was starting to draw. With his pen scratching to and fro, he bent muttering over his task. Gradually, as if in an artistic challenge for children, a sign of some kind took shape upon his pad, a beacon, perhaps, or a buoy. But which?

If this was an impromptu test it was a tricky one. Worried, I wracked my brains through the canal insignia. Unprepared, I had failed completely to swot these up. Happily, before I could blurt anything out, Monsieur Bertrand told me what this was himself. It was the symbol for a *tabac*, the double cone, nowadays made of plastic, displayed outside those shops. In the *tabac*, he explained, if I paid thirty-eight francs fifty, they would give me a *timbre fiscal*, a tax stamp. Pay for one of those, he declared, drop it in to the secretary, and the licence would be put in the post. Then, with a look that said very clearly 'Try not to bother me again' he turned to the other papers on his desk.

What was needed, still, was a bus. Back in England Bob had carried on looking. And at last, through the *demi-monde*, a second-hand one had emerged. Like Chris's machine it was a Ford Transit, but with stripes on the bodywork. There were headrests as well and even a certificate, a permit issued by the Manchester Traffic Area Office for Goods & Public Service Operator Licensing (a circumspect body, incidentally, not given to cosy consultations on the phone). How meaningful this might be was difficult to tell, but it could well prove useful in the roadside checks the Gendarmerie would be springing once the weather got better.

Two characters from the Wythenshawe Estate brought the bus out. A pack of turkey sandwiches, prepared by the driver's mum, had sustained them through the journey down, and they still had enough, so they insisted, to get them back to England now. 'Stay for a while,' we invited. But no: the call of home was greater, even if it involved the Dunkerque ferry. Some francs were handed over; then, as quickly as they could they departed.

This happened at Montargis, on our way towards the Seine, after which, wiser now to the delays on the Yonne, we would be travelling without passengers before taking on the first group at Auxerre. The bus we would retrieve when we could. Philip Streat, who was working for us now, could share in this, returning to it on a bike when needed or, if the timetable fitted, taking the local train.

We had, at the outset, employed a couple to work for us, Bob and I having met them several times in Manchester. Possibly married, possibly not - people were coy about that then - they were chosen in the notion they could develop into mine-host figures, a him-and-her double act which might row the show along - and give me time to think. It was not to be, and they did not stay for long.

Employment of couples, we were to find, is a dodgy business unless they have shared a vessel before. The closeness of the quarters and lack of privacy can come as a shock. Mannerisms that might in the wider world pass without consequence are all the more noticeable when you are with your partner throughout the day.

It was a help, to be honest, that they left so quickly, for it allowed Philip to join us instead, as an escape from the work he had been doing on Stanley and Jarrett's *Janine*. Already known to us, Philip was a far safer bet. On the *Janine* apparently, despite the ostentation of that vessel and the comforts for its passengers, he had to sleep in the laundry cupboard.

Why have a bus at all? It had not been part of the plan. Much of the pleasure, for me, is to be shot of such things. But not for our passengers. They wanted to see chateaux, and Vézelay, plus a winemaker's cellar, and anyway they had to be brought from Paris. So a bus it had to be, to be washed, and tinkered with, and taken to the tyre place, and explained to policemen, with tax discs and the suggestion that, in France at any rate, we ought to have a bus-operating company in order to be running it at all. Then there were the bicycles with which to retrieve it, the mud they splashed about, the punctures they suffered when you said you would get back quickly - and the headwinds.

Later, having found one at 150 francs, we bought a second-hand motor bike for these journeys. This meant a can to mix its fuel in, a plank so it could be wheeled inside the bus, rags to mop up the mess and yet more paperwork. There was a crash-helmet also, a massive thing, since it had to fit all sizes. When we employed the girl known as Mighty Min, a slender being, apparently built of fuse-wire, with a determination that belied her frame, she looked like a lolly on a stick.

The helmet, kept beneath the sink in the crew's quarters, would emerge at inconvenient moments, to roll around in the shower tray. It was useful to Philip once, however, when the door jammed, and he could put it on, to head-butt his way to freedom.

In the days when the French phone network was difficult to identify, the Nivernais had a separate system of its own. In the lock-houses higher up, heavy brass plugs would be inserted into sockets, then a handle whirled to make the connection. In my very early days I was privileged to overhear the following conversation:

'Hello, is that Lock 25?'

'Hold on a moment. I'm just dealing with a chicken.' A cackling noise, suddenly arrested, confirmed this remark.

'We've got a boat coming through tomorrow. Is there enough water in the cutting?'

'Well, the cellar's just flooded, so there should be.'

It was here that we first met The Whizzer. He was just a young lad then, a lanky, gangling figure in a peaked fishermen's cap, standing at the water's edge, looking perkily about. 'Chuck us a rope then,' he called, then whacked it round a railing, bringing us to such a sudden and shuddering halt that an elderly lady from Washington State, rising from her folding chair, capsized back with a cry. The Whizzer, meanwhile, pulled a Mars bar from his pocket. 'Lunch,' he remarked with a grin. 'All we have time for on that Hellship of ours.'

The Whizzer, it turned out, was waiting for the *Canard*, on which he served as odd-job man and general sorter of chores. Like ourselves, and many in the crew of *Palinurus*, he was British. To the bafflement of the canal staff and the perplexity of shopkeepers, whose pleasure at the increase in trade was complicated by people asking for Cheddar cheese and Marmite, such traffic as arrived was largely provided by Brits. (It is a preponderance that continues to this day. While there are now French nationals boating on their own canals, it remains an enthusiasm in which British people predominate, as happened with skiing in the Alps).

As deck-sweeper, rope-twirler, and occasional waiter at table, The Whizzer enjoyed what on any vessel is the most varied job of all - that of *matelot*, as the French put it, or deckhand. The other work on the *Canard* was done by Jimmy, the Captain, who drove the mini-bus as well, and by Clara, who cooked. With just a small number of passengers, the *Canard* could pass as a 'yacht', supposedly for private use only, exempt from registration, or the need for a licensed steerer.

As a further advantage, the *Canard*, unburdened by concrete, had been able to arrive from the south. Entering the Canal du Nivernais at Decize, she had been entirely free of the problems of depth that so restricted our own passage.

None of those on board the *Canard* was the owner. This was Isambard, a patrician figure back in England. Having toured the waterways on his own account, Isambard, who had other concerns, was putting the *Canard* out to charter, with Jimmy, Clara, and The Whizzer to run her.

For Jimmy, like the lads who had brought out the bus, France was a mysterious land. Such chores as shopping or negotiating a taxi took on for him the status of a diplomatic mission. It was as if, on meeting the locals, gifts of beads ought to be exchanged. Jimmy was careful. Under his captaincy, handling the *Canard* became akin to manoeuvring a battleship into Gibraltar. To The Whizzer, who was more of the rally-driving mentality, such prudence bordered on the unbearable.

Nor did it save them from incident. Travelling the opposite way to us, coming over the summit then down towards Auxerre, they had just had a major one. Relying heavily on Isambard's notes, their caution had been extreme. It was as if, as The Whizzer put it, they were working their way through a minefield. At each and every step they looked at the strip-map, with the boss's handwriting on it, to gather the latest advice. And there, one day, on the next page to come, was the expression 'Low Bridge'. Before this, though, was 'Very Low Bridge!' Then, nearer still, in fact a bridge they would encounter very soon, came the biggest obstacle of all. On the map, as emphatically as he could, Isambard had written 'Extremely Low Bridge!!!!' The 'Extremely' was heavily underlined.

Unlike *Secunda*, with which we had long given up, the *Canard* kept her wheelhouse assembled, up near the stern. Against both rain and sun it acted as a shield for the steerer and, at night-time, a boudoir for The Whizzer. In there, his evening's work done, he could grind his teeth at the day's longueurs and read the adventure novels and wartime reminiscences to which he was addicted.

At the first of the critical bridges the *Canard* eased into the gap. The Extremely Low Bridge with the triple underlinings compelled the utmost care. 'Yes, No, Yes,' cried The Whizzer, looking aft from the bow as the *Canard*, teetering slowly forward, advanced towards the crunch. In the event, there was room enough to spare, without even taking off the hooter or the other bits and pieces up on the wheelhouse roof. In safety *Canard* passed beneath the arch. Encouraged and relieved, Jimmy softened enough to allow The Whizzer an extra glass of Pepsi-Cola - a privilege in acknowledgement of their feat.

A similar success took place at the 'Very Low Bridge' that followed, causing Jimmy to relax enough at the last one to smash the wheelhouse to smithereens.

'There weren't many pieces bigger than we might have put in the stove,' The Whizzer explained in the course of this tale. 'The water level must have been up. Crazy. We had to patch up Jimmy as well. Sticking plaster all over the place. Made him look like a mummy. Ah, here, he comes…' Bumbling around the bend, the *Canard*, long and low, was finally revealed. 'I'm sleeping in a tent tonight,' The Whizzer was saying as, having cast off, we eased our way past the oncoming ship. She was, indeed, going extremely slowly. Jimmy, plastered still, was whirling the wheel as if in command of a windjammer running before a hurricane. Slowly and carefully our craft slid by one another, metal to metal, as barges are able to do.

The Whizzer stepped onto *Canard* again as she passed. Then, as we parted, he gazed back and waved. 'Look out for The Book,' he called.

'The what?'

There was a grin on his face. 'The Book!' he shouted. 'They keep it up near La Coudray.' On that mysterious note, he disappeared below to help with the supper.

Our crew member Mighty Min had fanciful ideas about the canal above Clamecy. The route now was narrow and constrained. 'Ooh,' Min remarked, as *Secunda* made her way through a tree-enshrouded portion beyond Tannay, 'Creepy! Do you think we'll meet the Monster in the Hat?' She had found, amongst the books on board, an almanac of cautionary tales with illustrations in a period style. In one of these, two children are approaching a large pointed hat, apparently left on the path through a wood. Next, just over the page, they discover that the hat has a wearer, a ghastly, witch-like presence underneath, rising through a hole in the ground.

This terrifying image, enough to give adults nightmares, became, after Min's remarks, so strongly identified with this part of the canal that none of us wanted to moor there. This time, though, as the lock-keeper's closing hour approached, we would have little choice.

'Do you know anything about The Book,' I asked as the last lock of the day gradually filled. We were near La Coudray now, but the woman looked nonplussed.

Perhaps my French was still not good enough; but the word *livre*, for book, was surely straightforward?

There was a new man in charge of the canal, we had heard, intent on cleaning up the act. The Book, maybe, was an official one, a ledger in which the misdemeanours of those in boats were recorded, such as mooring to trees, which was forbidden, or travelling too quickly, which, though also forbidden, verged on the impossible here. On a portion of the Canal De l'Est, visited in the *Arthur* several years before, just such a record had been kept, of every mortal infraction that could possibly be conceived: such as driving in mooring spikes on the towpath side, as opposed to the impenetrable jungle opposite; running your engine after 8pm; taking off mooring ropes before lock-gates were *fully* open; and so on. On-the-spot fines were levied by the area foreman and his rhino-like wife, who lived in suspicious splendour by the waterside.

The mariner's equivalent of the Naughty Book? It did not sound a Nivernais thing.

We stopped that evening within view of some fields, Philip winding the ropes round the trees, which, however unacceptable under the rules, was the only means of mooring here. On the Nivernais, we found, the banks could be too crumbly for spikes, while surges in the water, which happen on even the quietest of canals, pulled them out again anyway.

To stop at the end of the day, even under these circumstances, with the smells of food to be served, a glass of wine waiting, was a great, great feeling. There were just a few jobs to be done. After tightening in the ropes, we could fiddle with the gangplank. The main job, once it was pushed into position (a manoeuvre which was a cross between running with a battering-ram and launching a bobsleigh) was to stop it squeaking as the boat moved about. Even on a canal this will happen as water wafts by, pushed very often by the wind, or a sluice leaking somewhere.

'Let's leave it,' I said to Phil, 'and go and have a drink.'

Squeeeeak …

'You think so? Oh, OK.'

Grauuuuu …ch.

Muttering under our breath we pulled it back in. Which was as well, as it proved.

A breeze sprang up, becoming chilly as Philip, on washing-up duty, switched off the lights and made for bed.

Then the noises started. Indistinct at first, they were little more than a shuffling, as if the leaves that shook in the wind were somehow now metallic. From across the fields it came, the sound of ghostly armour, faint then sharper, then fading yet again. Peering hard revealed nothing. With the nearest village a kilometre away, its houses shuttered, there was just the blackness of night-time rural France.

Mighty Min, I learned later, had risen during the night, slid back a window to listen, then gone for a ramble round the barge. She was found in the morning back in her bunk, wearing the helmet we used for the motor bike, with the mooring spike mallet by her hand.

In daylight all was revealed. Out on the path, in all its hideous glory, was an animal. With a curling lip and penetrating stare, it was also very large. It was, to borrow James Thurber's expression, piano-shaped, albeit a piano covered in hair. The hair was unkempt, the gaze unsympathetic. A length of chain hung from its neck, to rattle when it moved. From its direction, since we were downwind, came an eye-watering odour.

At last I realised the meaning of The Whizzer's expression. He was good at French, I discovered, having in his brief but action-packed career been with a theatre group elsewhere in the land. Out of mischief, however, he spoke with a strong English accent. 'Look out for The Book,' he had said. It was not a book at all, but *un bouc*, a prime example of the same. It was a billy-goat.

No-one went for bread that morning. Instead we served rusks with an alternative use, perhaps, as household insulation. The old lady from Washington apart, who plainly had trouble with them, our passengers accepted these stoically and gnawed their way through breakfast. As compensation there was Oxford marmalade, which Portia brought with her on one of the visits that she made. As she explained, 'there may be wonderful food in France, but they haven't much idea about breakfast. The tea's like dishwater and they get their marmalade mixed up with jam.'

With a whirring noise, a motor scooter appeared on the opposite side. It was the lock-keeper arriving, a *remplaçant*, or temporary hand, for the cottage had fallen into disrepair and there was no regular person here. There were two locks ahead, a short distance apart, and the *remplaçent*, male for a change, would be working them both. Seconded from the maintenance staff, he had drawn the short straw in the roster of duties. The *bouc*, responding to this new source of interest, trotted off towards him. Seizing this opportunity we could cast off the ropes, to head towards the lock.

The keeper was a small man, round and perspiring. Dressed in *bleus de travail* with a beret to complete the picture, he was in many respects the classic country *ouvrier*. Not for him, though, the leisurely style of that stoical group of men. This was a hero, Clark Kent in disguise.

Rarely have gates been opened so quickly. Rarely do figures such as these leap down upon a boat as she is entering - from a considerable height in this case. It was if one of the Mistermen had arrived. 'Beware of that animal,' he said with unnecessary fervour. 'It is *méchant*. And, yes, it hurts.' The *Bouc*, wrong-footed by this manoeuvre, showed fresh intent when our man shinned up the ladder on the farther side. In the fashion of the largest of the Billy Goats Gruff it made its way over the other set of gates. 'You work the locks,' the keeper called over his shoulder. 'Quick as you can, mind. I'll lead it away, while you do.'

Not so much a lock-keeper, he was more of a decoy, appearing unexpectedly at one point out of the rhubarb-like vegetation that lay alongside, enjoining us, as ever, to get on with it.

On his scooter again, he came whirring past later, mopping his brow symbolically as he headed for the local café. Whatever he chose to drink there he deserved it. The *Bouc*, we were to learn, was known as a scourge of this area. A truculent farmer owned it and whenever he fell out with the foreman of this stretch (not a difficult thing to do, it has to be added) he would station this beast in order to harass the staff.

'Tell me about it,' said The Whizzer the next time we met him. 'Almost got in the saloon when we went through. Chewed the sun-umbrellas and shat all over the side-deck.' The Whizzer liked adventures, we were to discover, and when life did not provide them tended to invent his own. 'Turned the fire-extinguisher on him in the end. Nasty. This canal's hard enough work as it is.'

Near here, at Tannay, we paid a visit to Madame Moreau. Courteous and dignified, Madame Moreau made wine, a rarity now in this region, some distance as it is from the favoured slopes of Chablis. And always, on visiting here, there were glimpses of earlier worlds, not least that of her late husband Georges, a remarkable figure who, in a role more definite than the mysteries of Pierre, ran the Resistance unit Le Loup. Based in the woods south of Clamecy at the spot known as La Cage aux Loups, The Wolves' Cage, it had taken its name from there. After building up the wine business once the war was over, Georges Moreau died in 1974, leaving his family to carry on the enterprise.

Our interest provoked by such little as we had heard of the Resistance - if naïvely so, with a *Boy's Own Paper* slant to it - we would ask her for details. And a few were forthcoming, but only in outline, with a willingness always to change the subject. No, she did not seem to know Pierre; at least, when we asked, she showed no particular interest. Maquis members operated under pseudonyms, she pointed out. They could be difficult to trace.

Hers may not have been the greatest of wines, but there was something about each visit that was beguiling. It was a glimpse into the days before wine became big business, when there were vineyards in many areas, kept to serve local needs. Only after phylloxera, the insect that in the 1870s killed virtually all the vines, were the vineyards in Europe ripped up. Then after the discovery that American root-stock was immune, replanting took place, but selectively, leaving regions such as the Yonne for the larger part devoid of grapes. Tannay, with its revived vineyards, was special and a visit there, getting beyond the gloss of so much wine presentation, was always rewarding.

On the activities of the Resistance Madame Moreau gave us a photocopied sheet, listing the ambushes and the shoot-outs in which Maquis Le Loup had been involved. Pierre, however, remained unexplained.

7: LOOKING FOR MONEY

Already, the 'new' bus was beginning to play up. Under the accumulated weight of fourteen passengers, miraculously attracted as a group from Oklahoma, together with their baggage, the springs on one side were sagging. From the back axle, too, sticky grease was escaping. Whoever at the Traffic Area Office in Manchester awarded the magical ticket had clearly been no clairvoyant. A series of electrical mysteries made the latest visit to Paris a harrowing one.

'Ladies and gentlemen,' I declared at the hotel where we met our clients, 'I'm sorry to be so late but we had a small problem on the way. Please do not concern yourselves; it's all fixed now.' Somehow, I sensed, I could have been more cautious. 'We have a three hour journey ahead of us, so please make yourselves comfortable.'

Amongst the dreams that visit me from time to time, one is of being a student, with exams imminent and an impossible amount of swotting still to be done. Another sets itself on the expressway beside the Seine in Paris with the engine mysteriously dead and a busload of people wondering why they paid to get into such a mess. During waking hours both have actually happened.

'Ahem, we appear to have a fault, ladies and gentlemen. Excuse me for a moment while I take a look.' Pulled in beside the barrier, with traffic hurtling by, I remember thinking what a good job it was we did not pursue one of the dafter resolutions at our director-shareholder's meetings - that we should paint the company name on the side. With the bonnet lifted I wiped a few things, tweaked a wire on which the insulation had partially melted, then, before the apprehensive throng, climbed in to try the ignition. Miraculously, the engine started up again, then continued to run.

It would do this wholeheartedly, I was to discover, only with my foot flat to the boards. Anything less, and it started to miss again. 'You're early,' the crew declared with indignation as I bowled up beside them. They had only just finished getting the boat ready, and had not had time to change.

'I didn't have much choice,' I told them. 'If we'd stopped at all, I'm not sure we could have started again.'

Expenditure by now was critical. Try as Bob might - and the Oklahoman group was a major coup - bookings for *Secunda* were not keeping up. Somehow or other we managed to continue. I remember spending the cash given as tips to pay for the laundry.

Beside the bonfire one night, an elderly passenger gave me the benefit of his wisdom. I had not described to him our predicament, or even spoken of our worries. Probably, they were evident enough: in the state of our bus, for example, or the way we were running short of towels.

He was another of those who spoke extremely slowly. More an American characteristic than a British, it conceals very often, as remarked upon before, an extremely agile mind. As a businessman of experience, he had analysed our set-up and, as he was leaving, dropped into my ear the recommendation on which it all hung.

In the meantime, as he explained, 'There are many factors that make a successful business.' Then he listed some. It took a little time. 'But the biggest single one is …' There was, of course, a further pause before the all-important word.

'… luck,' was what he said.

Luck? We needed some of that. Once that cruise was over, we had a gap of a few days *sans passagers* but, regrettably, *sans argent* also. The bus, at a garage for attention, would soak up much of the cash that was left. As to the boat, we were up at Baye again, that blessed venue at which, all too often, there were too many bothersome thoughts to allow full enjoyment of the place.

As ever, the others in our crew were making better use of their time. An expedition had been mounted in our dinghy down the Rigole. This is a high, narrow channel, running for thirty-odd kilometres from Pannesière to the east to keep the Canal du Nivernais topped up with water. A feat of engineering on its own, the Rigole provides a one-day voyage in a dinghy, borne on the current. That it joins the main canal unexpectedly in a waterfall took our party by surprise, but it was a warm evening and they recovered from it quickly.

Exuberant though they were, I was too beset by anxiety to join them, having spent much of that day constructing a detailed cash-flow. It was a real one again, not some work of fiction. The results were intensely discouraging. I would need to telephone Bob.

It is odd today to recall those times in France when the public phone box was such a rarity that many a township did not have one at all. What you did was go to a post office or a bar, preferably the post office, since bars would double the price. And there you booked a call. A stunned and prolonged silence greeted the news that this would be to England. Then, hesitantly, with many a look at the number, the soul behind the counter would attempt to make contact with the operator.

Back, eventually, came the news as to how long you had to wait. A delay of an hour was round about standard, but could easily be as many as three. Once, when there was a strike going on, the waiting time was nine hours, which was absolutely useless. In any case the lady at the exchange in Corbigny, where I was phoning from now, checked out early in the evening. From that time onwards the town was effectively cut off. At weekends or public holidays making any kind of call was too difficult to be tried.

In the 1980s all this was to change. In a sweeping programme of reforms, telephone cabins were put up all over the land. Sometimes, even, there was one beside a lock. And when, a couple of years later those who planned this system grasped that it might be useful to display the numbers in the boxes, it even became possible to say you were running out of change, then ask to be telephoned back. But these innovations had yet to come.

This time in Corbigny there was only a forty minute delay, which meant I might actually get through in the window of opportunity in which the post office might be open while Bob or Hector were at their desks.

In such a fraught situation it was important to be brief. 'Hi,' I would say, 'Have you sent the money yet?' to be followed by heartfelt thanks - or a muttered expression of dismay. The negative response, alas, was all too common. 'Sorry, John, I can't'

And that, this time, was what was said. No, they could not send any money. There was no more money left to send.

Back in England things had been ugly. Bob, convening a meeting in my absence, found himself holding back the furies. We should close down immediately, it was said - regardless of obligation to those already booked. Or, others declared, we should go on our hands and knees to Stanley, to beg him for customers. Maybe, even, at a rock-bottom price, we might sell *Secunda* to him. Further members still seemed to think - on the grounds we had got this far - that somehow we might survive.

With several weeks voyaging yet to do, there was enough in the bank in France and in my wallet, I calculated, to get us through the next ten days. Then? It hardly bore thinking about.

It was the Cortina that I would be driving down to Nevers, to visit our bank and recover such francs as remained. There was a cycle ride first to reach this machine, over the hill then down to Chitry.

Never had the countryside seemed so vivid. In times of stress the perception sharpens. Whenever there was a crisis, or when there were passengers due, which always stretched the nerves, how attractive did the idea become of turning one's back on it all, for a stroll down the path, admiring the butterflies and flowers, the vistas of woodland and meadow - and to never come back. It was the tension, perversely, that increased the appreciation.

This is one of the finest cycle rides of all time. First of all out of Baye and along the path that the mules used to take, while their barges, astern of a tug, were towed through the tunnels. There, on the crest of the hill, is the old engineer's house by a short wide tower, built around the vent shaft from the tunnel. A cottage follows, beside the quarry, overgrown now, where Chris once found the old canal records, dumped when the office was moved to Corbigny. Then, beyond the cuttings, the path descends at last, to join the waterway again, by the first in the long flight of locks towards Auxerre.

It was here, whenever there might be a boat around, that Pierre would emerge, blinking, with his wartime bit of paper. Then, along the spectacular straight known as the Tranchée de La Chaise, a succession of bridges stood high, as in a mirage. The sun was shining. Birds soared as ever; wild flowers shifted their colours as I pedalled. But I was on my way to the bank.

Changing from bike to car, I headed now for Nevers. The southern side of these hills remains remote to this day. Wonderfully un-mucked-about, this is *La France profonde des campagnes*, steady and serene. At the village of St-Saulge I picked up a hitch-hiker.

Plenty of people hitch-hiked in that part of France. It was, and to some extent still is, an accepted means of getting around. It helped, of course, to look youthful and keen, with an honest expression. A college scarf was a plus - those who seriously needed a lift, maybe older and unable to afford a razor, being far less likely to get one. The character I picked up that day lay somewhere in between. Untidy and monosyllabic he was, by coincidence, travelling to a spot the other side of Nevers, close to Marseilles-lès-Aubigny, where I intended going on afterwards, to collect the mail. We would call at the bank on the way.

Nevers, a pleasant enough city, is a city all the same. It seemed sensible there not to leave my companion waiting in the car. He might not have been the kind of guy who would prise out the radio in my absence, but he could have been. So I took him into the bank with me. There he would wait with other spectators while I queued at the counter.

There was always something daunting about the bank. Maybe our parlous finances were responsible. Perhaps it was the airs and graces of the staff, which varied, but it was hardly a charm school.

Possibly it was the fact that, despite our being in business over a year, they had yet to grant us a cheque-book. The reason for this, apparently, was our company structure, rooted as it was in Britain. The Chamber of Commerce at Bourges would look into the matter from time to time. Then they put the file away again. Being half-way there, so to speak, we got half the facilities of the bank.

For us every outgoing had to be conducted in cash, to be collected, when available, by means of a personal visit, with perusals of passport and many a suspicious glare. While this, today, might well seem absurd, procedures then were on a par with the telephone: laborious, limited and determinedly local.

Off-putting also had been the formality of French documentation, in which the positive and negative, heavily intertwined, would be clouded with warnings, references to the numbers of sundry laws, and threats of prosecution. Whatever the cause, banks had - and to this day still have - a terrible effect on my French. Lapsing, as ever when stressed, into a Manchester accent, I explained to the clerk my purpose. Brows furrowing, he went to a filing cabinet to look up the details of our account.

This was a bothersome moment. Supposing, through one of the technicalities with which the system increasingly bristled, I would be denied any withdrawal at all: how could we run the boat? Rabbit, possibly, might be served up for supper, to be bartered from a lock-keeper in exchange for surplus paint. Charges for drinks at the bar, reintroduced, might win us a little more cash, enough to put fuel in the tanks.

The bank clerk certainly took his time. There was a paper in the file, which he stared at for an age. Then, to drag out the suspense, he carried it over to someone else. For an even longer time the pair of them studied it. They glanced in my direction, stared at it again, then the older one nodded. The clerk approached once more, the paper in his hand.

'It seems,' he began, 'there has been a something or other.' He spoke too quickly. It was hard to follow. 'This paper,' he continued, 'is from the *Douane* ...'

Fingers trembling, I reached out to take it from him. The *Douane*, the French customs, before whom the highest in the land thought it sensible to grovel, had decided after all that we owed them more than we'd paid. Despairingly I glanced back at the hitch-hiker, sitting not too far behind. He did not look the kind of man who might advance us a loan right now.

There was nothing for it but to examine the paper more closely. How much did the bastards want? It seemed to be a lot, a substantial sum indeed. Then, slowly, light began to dawn. This was not money they 'wanted'. *Secunda* having been in France for whatever time such things took, they were proposing to give it back to us. The import duty the *Douane* had charged could now be returned. Not only could it, the clerk was saying, it had been. The entire sum was there, in the bank, waiting, forty-odd thousand francs, a massive amount in those days. It was enough to see us through - and more.

It was unbelievable. 'Sign here,' said the clerk. I could have kissed him. We were saved.

There was still a little drama to come, a scrap of panto to round things off. Under the peculiarities of our arrangement, cash was the only means of withdrawal, a bit at a time for preference, though technically, if we wanted, in its entirety.

Indecent though it looked, it struck me forcibly that we should do this straight away, that very moment, before those who were holding our cash thought of bank-type reasons for changing their minds. Better some embarrassment now than seriously going bust.

Trying not to shake, I totted up the total. We had over forty thousand francs. This was serious stuff, a windfall equivalent to the purchase price of *Secunda* herself, during those early days in the Netherlands.

'Yes,' I said. 'We'll have it now.' Looking startled, as well he might, the clerk gazed to the farther end of the counter. There, reminiscent of the time when visitors to banks arrived there with ponies and traps, the cashier sat in a booth made of heavy-duty glass, counting out such cash as people might require. It was to him that you went after your dealings at the counter, bearing a slip of paper for his attention. It was a very old system.

The clerk, however, was not a formalities man. 'Hey,' he bellowed up the hall, 'Jacques! Have you got forty-six thousand francs?'

There was silence in the building. 'How much?' Jacques shouted back. There was incredulity in his voice.

'Forty-six thousand,' our man began again. He pointed at me. 'Forty-six thousand, three hundred and twenty-seven. For this chap here,' he continued, making sure everyone knew.

'*Phouaff*,' exclaimed Jacques. He may have said '*Zut alors*' as well; certainly there was a range of Gallic gesture, eye-rolling included and the slapping of a hand to the forehead. I concentrated on looking determined. A delay then took place in which any of the other customers who wanted money were obliged to wait as Jacques set off back-stage, presumably to go to the vaults.

There was quite an audience for his return. Muttering, he counted it out: 'Two thousand ..., four thousand ..., six. Hang on a minute.' And so on. At the end the bundle of notes, now huge, was shoved across at me through a slot in the watch-tower,

This did not seem proper 'Have you got an envelope?' I asked him.

'A what?'

'An envelope. To put this money in.'

'*Phouaff*' said Jacques again. Whatever next, he was plainly thinking, will this extremely demanding customer want?

After some digging around an envelope was produced into which the money could be stuffed. There were even more bystanders by then, to many of whom such a sum represented around nine month's wages.

Sticking the envelope down my shirt, I drove the hitch-hiker as directly as possible to his rendezvous. Had he attempted robbery the guy could have ruined us; but he only wanted to see his girlfriend. Without comment he disembarked, for all the world as if he had been given a lift in the bread van. I salute him.

Some years later, when a tax inspector reviewed our accounts, he came across this item. 'A mistake,' he said. 'You were not entitled to that back.' No, he went on, they did not require it now. Too much time had expired. It was beyond the statutory limit. 'You were lucky,' he said. We certainly were.

The firework display came not long afterwards. The fireworks in Auxerre were a major attraction. Staged by the waterside each summer, they drew in the crowds from many miles around. Bands played, loudspeaker announcements rattled round the houses, the gendarmerie stood by on a three-line whip. Then it began: rockets, golden rain, the lot. Aerial grenades thudded against the eardrums. Flares shot into the sky as pets throughout the city howled in collective pain. After a fusillade threatening a communal nose-bleed, the event concluded with the apparent combustion of the cathedral.

To watch this from the river was a treat and a half. *Secunda* could not be present, but the *Escargot* was, her captain, Jim Page, manipulating their schedule to be in pole position for the night. He invited us down to join him.

Watching with us also were Jimmy and Clara from the *Canard*, though not The Whizzer. Having friends in the city with whom he might stay, he had come to Auxerre already. Jimmy and Clara, though, would be travelling back to Baye with us. The bus, repaired and paid for at last, provided our transport for the night.

The fireworks, as ever, had been excellent. The *Escargot*, with her enormous foredeck, gave us the kind of seating millionaires vie for at the equivalent event in Monaco. The drive back from Auxerre to Baye could be accomplished in just over an hour, the roads becoming empty as the city was left behind. By Clamecy, around the half-way mark, we were out there on our own. It was ten minutes beyond that the smell of burning made itself felt. The garage, though fixing the electrics, had failed to look at the cooling.

Jimmy, who liked the certainties of life, was the last person really to send off in search of water, but Philip and I were preoccupied at the time, trying in the darkness to trace the source of the leak.

There was a village nearby, towards which Jimmy wandered, then rattled the gate of the very first house. A meeting with a lurcher followed. Other dogs began barking as well. Lights came on. Tongue-tied at the best of times, Jimmy returned with a brigand-like individual at his elbow who, in the interest of seeing us gone, provided a bottle filled with water. Brought out in his dressing gown, he looked to some degree out of sorts. Next, after noticing the number plate on our bus, he became anti-foreigner as well. Any repeats, it was plain, would not be well received.

When the motor heated up again Philip found us a stream. After that, Mighty Min, staring through the rear window, would watch the trail on the tarmac, then shout when the water dried up.

By contrast with England where even after midnight few roads go untravelled, not a single vehicle came by to give succour. Out in the wilderness, with mists beginning to gather, we would stumble into ditches, cursing the smallness of the bottle.

Almost at journey's end, with the Moon up, we stood once again by the roadside. Above, as so often here, the stars were out in swathes. There are many parts of the world, no doubt, where the skies match those of Burgundy; but for me, as ever, this was magic. As we waited, yet again, for the motor to cool off, someone noticed the stone. There, right beside where we were parked, stood this short wide slab with a rounded top. There was lettering on it. Our torch, almost as tired as ourselves, could just pick it out.

There was a name, a date in 1944, and the starkest of messages. 'Assassinated by the Germans'. Here, in the middle of nowhere? How? And why? None of us said anything. Untouched by war ourselves it had been easy to be lightly curious about the regime of Marshal Pétain, or the faintly farcical sight of Pierre, cadging a drink by the lock-side. But in this starlit countryside, under who knew what circumstance, someone, possibly someone younger than ourselves, had been put by the roadside and shot. When, at last, we got to the boat again, we all went quietly to bed.

Often, with our passengers, we would visit the *chateau* nearby, a splendid house with battlements, rising grandly through the trees. Amongst the seventeenth Century furnishings, Aubusson tapestries, and the paintings of sibyls, the owner, a retired army general and ex-ambassador to Sweden, would lead the party round. There was an aura about these visits, a sense of being there as an extended family member, not least when stumbling upon some real family member in the drawing room, slumbering after lunch.

Other features of the *chateau* were the possibilities of being torn to pieces by the resident dog ('Keep still! He's just a little excited. Oh, he does not seem to like you!') and the tendency to employ English public schoolboys to look after the *châtelain*'s horses. 'Madeleine,' a young man bellowed as he crashed into the room where we were intently studying the murals, 'What are these dweadful stains on my jodhpurs? Weally! It's too bad. You should have put them thwew the laundwy.'

Beyond the walls of the chateau, rustic France was still to be found. There, at a lock I had better not name, was old Uncle Henri who, though he generally sat outside the family cottage with scarcely a move, suddenly became motivated one day to rush towards *Palinurus* with a shotgun under his arm.

Trapped as they were in the lock, those on deck took cover. The competition to get behind a picnic table, we heard, was particularly keen. It was a relief to all concerned to see this figure, like Chaplin in a mime-show, execute a right-angled turn, then disappear inside a shed. A succession of reports then followed. Shards of tile pattered down as Madame, waiting for an even number of shots, seized the interval of reloading to drag him out again. 'It was a snake,' she reported later. A grass-snake, probably, living an otherwise blameless life, it had been spotted in the rafters and, since the citizens of Nièvre are incapable of distinguishing between vipers, which are mildly venomous, and the species that are not, it had to be hunted down.

Whether Uncle Henri got it or not remained unclear. When we next went by, there he was, sitting on his bench again, like one of those people who cover themselves in spray-paint and pretend to be statues. It seemed a good idea, all the same, to get through as quickly as we could.

Drink would be at the bottom of these incidents; wine very often, sometimes pastis, but, once in a while absinthe. Absinthe, illegal in France, was still being produced in these woods. As the one-time drink of preference amongst the literati, from Verlaine through to Hemingway, it retained that mystique for years. On the Nivernais it is rarely encountered now, but in *Secunda*'s early days, stubble-chinned gentlemen with a conspiratorial look would stumble towards the lockside, tapping their noses in anticipation.

Sticky and green, absinthe owes its hallucinatory properties to wormwood. Its prohibition, which has not extended to every country, can be attributed to a ghastly incident in Switzerland in 1905 when a man slaughtered his family.

Phil Baker's *Daedalus Book of Absinthe* is an authority on the matter, pointing out that, despite the murderer working his way through a massive list of beverages beforehand, it was absinthe alone that the Swiss chose to ban. The French government followed in 1915 'scapegoating it,' according to the author, 'for the national alcohol problem and for the French army's unreadiness for the First World War.' As with marihuana, its illegality seems to have added to the mystique.

I have tried it a few times, most notably at the hands of Peter Zivy, the pioneer hire-boat operator who, by setting up in business at Baye, effectively saved the Canal. He poured us far too much and, at the end of a supper that included pigeon, I was hallucinating.

Drunkenness, or the effect of it, is easily forgotten. So when, whilst steering *Secunda,* a member of the maintenance staff waved a bottle at me, I accepted. There may not have been much maintenance done, but it did not do to be stand-offish.

To quote a jokey poster which Michael Streat once wrote, excessive drinking by the captain is to be discouraged. He may see two bridges where only one exists; luckily, as he will also see two boats he only has to steer one through each.

The boost from alcohol, of course, can be illusory, which appears to be absinthe's problem. Because it contains a stimulant, it was deemed by a number of writers and painters, including Toulouse-Lautrec (who mixed it with brandy, which he carried in a hollow walking-stick) to be inspirational. For a time, maybe, this is so - before with further pourings it becomes destructive.

In my own case, after a bout of mindless chat, I handed over the wheel to Duncan. The cabin in the bow, if I could make it there, looked a good place to sleep. Never in the heat of the day the best spot to retire to, the slumber it provided, riven with thoughts of molten lava, recalled closely Peter Zivy's supper party those several years before. The government of 1915 might have been right after all.

Chris Ryle, by now, had sold the *Pisgah* to Tony Paris. Chris, with a family to support, would be going back to architecture in order to make a living. Tony, teacher at a private school, would run the *Pisgah* now in a style that, in our more put-upon moments, several of us wished we had adopted at the start. That is he operated without a permit to carry passengers, unbeknownst to the fiscal authorities, employment enforcers, gentlemen insisting on stability calculations, or hair-splitters over tax. If asked he could always protest he was there for his own amusement - for which, as already reported, many forms of bureaucratic control were miraculously waived - and in general he jogged along well enough.

Never, when he might be enjoying the view, did Tony have to work out Value Added Tax. Nor need he be bothered with the nuances of bus operation. People coming to his boat were expected to find it first of all, then arrange such excursions as they wished for themselves. To justify all this, his holidays were extremely cheap.

There were disadvantages to Tony nonetheless. One was his appalling boat handling which meant that when on the Yonne with him, where the locks are bigger and vessels have to share, there was every chance of being rammed or having lines thrown round panic-stricken passengers. Never, in his several years on waterways did Tony learn the old adage that in a tricky situation you slow right down or, if possible, stop. His was an all-shouting, engine-roaring scenario in which the ropes, should anyone manage to attach them, would be twanging away like banjo strings.

Technical know-how, generally, had never been Tony's strong point. For much of the time, since those on board were usually youth groups, there would be a supervisor coming too, who might have the togetherness to dip the oil or work out the need to change a filter. When there was no such saviour it paid the rest of us to be on our toes. 'Care for a glass of wine, John?' was the signal for a shot of Algerian plonk, accompanied by 'Know anything about water-pumps do you?' But, if we often tried to avoid him, in his freedom from what the French call *paperasse* we envied him as well.

There was one other vessel we saw from time to time, running outside the regulations also, but on a more sophisticated level. This was the *Campagnarde de Bourgogne*, and if Tony broke the rules in an absent-minded way, and was probably unaware of half of them, Eric James who ran the *Campagnarde*, knew exactly what he was doing. As big as the *Janine*, and therefore incapable of getting beyond the bridges at Auxerre, his was a vessel to reckon with. Spacious and luxurious, she had been put together in the Netherlands with a minimum of fuss, at a fraction of what Stanley had been paying; for Eric had a calculating mind.

Cool affluence was the theme of his operation. For his kind of client the routes did not matter; just the sound of them. Between Paris and Auxerre it is samey, to say the least - but the cabins were massive, for a handful of people only, paying extravagant amounts. The visits to wineries, or Fontainebleau, were made not in a bus, but in elegant if elderly limousines, picked up for a song in England. When the *Campagnarde* was in France she flew the Dutch flag, when in the Netherlands the French. Once, at least, Eric had changed her name.

If officials came aboard Eric asked them to leave. He paid the minimum of tax (as did we all, but none of us had the nerve that he had). In conversation he was urbane, but gave little away. On the vessel herself was a grand piano, and amongst the décor a huge Victorian portrait in oils, possibly retouched to suggest some kind of ancestry of Eric himself. In a way we were in awe of him, for the snobbery of the operation, the sheer sang-froid. But in the months to come Eric would land us well and truly in it.

Steering our own barge was always testing enough. Whereas in a car the wheel, which is light, is turned very little, on a barge it can be heavy, and is constantly on the move. Rarely is the vessel headed straight, certainly in a shallow canal, where the stern gets dragged one way or the other, so that, even with experience, there is constant correction going on.

On the plus side guiding a barge such as this got the helmsman extremely fit. It was not just the work behind the wheel, but the upping and downing at the locks, the winding of sluice handles, and the jumping ashore and back again. No gym can match it.

The bus, on the other hand, was taxing in other ways. 'Do not speak to the driver' a notice declared, but many people did. The ride back into Paris at the end of a cruise, with folk who may still have been clients, but had also become our friends, was one of mixed feelings. You got to know these people. They had become relaxed, and to a considerable extent dependent upon the Captain. For them as much as for us the canyons of the Boulevarde Peripherique, the awful inner road in Paris, signified the re-entry into stress. As they left and said their farewells they would have to take decisions again. 'Can you get us a taxi?' they still could be asking, something of which they were surely as capable as ourselves.

Whenever I did the bus trip, my very first urge, after saying the farewells, was to get out of Paris again, to somewhere with a pace more measured: Port Marly, perhaps, on the outskirts, maybe a place near Versailles, or the barge town down the Seine of Conflans-Sainte-Honorine. There in a little hotel, the kind that still had bolsters, apparently filled with sand, and a wardrobe modelled on the Arc de Triomphe, it would be possible to have a decent meal, read a book and, to a degree, wind down.

Then the following day, as the bus had to be washed, and the deadline approached, came the tension of meeting the next group of passengers. Would they be nice? Or demanding? Would they all be there? It could be horrendous tracking down those who were not. Would they have their luggage? Or would the airline/bus company/their last hotel have lost it? Tracing this could be difficult too. Then the weaving through Paris on the drive out to the expressway. 'What's that building there? Is it the Palace of Justice?' 'Does the barge have a hair-drier on board?' 'I think I may have left my purse!' If only each time a new group joined they could be overlapped with the old. Then they might have picked up the vibes and calmed themselves down a bit.

8: THE *DOUANE* INTERVENES

In the usual fashion each morning we would take it in turns to get the bread. 'The bread run,' as it was known, was a variable experience, ranging from jaunts on a bike, or even a leisurely stroll, to a quartering of the countryside in mounting stages of panic. This would usually be the case on a Monday, which many in the shop-owning fraternity in France spend with their premises closed.

While there are in France occasional bread shops on duty on Mondays these can be tricky to find. On such a day in September, around fifteen kilometres from Auxerre, it was my turn. Taking one of the push-bikes I explored the area round Vincelles.

There must be one somewhere. 'In Auxerre' a beaming lady told me in the village of Champs, as if that were good news. With fifteen minutes to cycle back to the boat, then another fifteen to get to Auxerre in the bus, I would be flying; but it had to be done. While our willing staff padded out breakfast with fruit juice and the explanation that, although the bread would be late, it was bound to be worth the wait, a chase into the city began.

Often in France I seemed the only person in a hurry. At any time during the week, at the post office or in the supermarket, there were families with their best clothes on. For them, apparently, shopping was a major occasion. At the bakery people in the queue stopped for a chat, fiddled around for change, dropped it, changed their minds about what they were ordering, then, mixing their farewells with news of the shortage of runner beans at Boudin-le-Noir, would start all over again. It is admirable. But, when your need is urgent, the lifestyle can be tiresome.

So it was in Auxerre. A stream of people, pottering along with sticks of bread beneath their armpits, provided signs of a *boulangerie*. Slamming to a stop at the kerbside, I joined the low-adrenaline line straggling out of the doorway. Beyond lay glimpses of what we needed. *Baguettes, croissants au beurre, pains au chocolat*, all seemed to be there. It was late maybe, but it was fresh. Then the fates struck.

A rap on the window of the bus attracted my attention to a foxy-looking character in a leather jacket. He had some kind of badge to show me. Perhaps he was from Health & Safety, gathering evidence on the bread trade and its failures in wrapping things up? A parking attendant? No, he was a customs officer in mufti, and he wanted to talk about our bus.

An examination of the papers followed, then consultation with a pal, as wide as the first man was thin. It was the same kind of pairing as we met back at Calais, one of them smiling, albeit weakly, the other one not. They would follow, they said, to wherever the bread was being taken. It was a barge, was it? That perked them up a good deal more.

So it was, on a glowing morning, with the mists just lifting and a zing in the air, that our guests, hungry for decent bread, had this pair of enforcers amongst them as well. You could, so it was said, deny police or customs officers the right to come on board 'a visiting ship,' a vessel from another country. Eric James might get away with it, and did; but for us this did not seem a good idea right now.

What these guys wanted to see now were the ship's papers, together with proof of importation. That we had this was a disappointment to them. Still, there was this matter of the bus … Operating a British bus in France, they explained, was illegal. British coach companies might be doing it when they brought their tourists over, but they were not allowed to stay and do it. At least not for long. Yes, it was acknowledged testily, it would have been alright if we were running the bus for our own amusement. But not if people were paying. We were back in the Bermuda Triangle again.

We were committing an infraction, the thin one declared. His companion nodded in agreement, darkened glasses flashing. We must import the vehicle forthwith, they said, and get French number plates. This was not good. Friends who had tried this process with their cars, co-operative at first, then finally in despair, reported on the obstacles in their path. Did the wiring, for example, conform to French requirements? The fuel system? The brakes? Verification from the manufacturers was required, printed out in French. In a protectionist society such as this, getting a foreign vehicle accepted was a challenge and a half.

Otherwise, it was sternly explained, we had a week to get the bus out of France. In the meantime there was a 2,000 Franc fine. I went to their office to sort this out; and that was the morning gone.

By this stage, there were five weeks of our season left to run. We needed a bus. There was neither time nor the wherewithal to find another one. No such vehicle with this number of seats, in France, was ever available for hire.

An hour or so in the post office got me a call through to Bob. Yes, he said, the bus would still be insured. In the short discussion following, we hatched up a plan to get us to the season's end. In the regions, we had noticed, those on official business stayed in their own patch. Canal officials in Nevers had nothing to do with their counterparts down the Yonne. These, in turn, had no apparent contact with Dijon. Customs officers, likewise, looked unlikely to be free-range. So, paying the fine and nodding dutifully, we went to the Canal de Bourgogne instead.

The township of Migennes, twenty or so kilometres north of Auxerre, is where the Canal de Bourgogne branches off. It is not the most tranquil of spots, since there are marshalling yards there as well, but it provided a haven from the Yonne which, on the way down, was starting to be muscular again.

As such, the Bourgogne - the Burgundy Canal - offers a return to the intimacy that the smaller waterways provide. But it does not come in a rush. Glorious though it is farther on, the first few hour's run provide something of a curate's egg.

As often with a canal from a flood plain, the initial parts are straight and long. With trains hurtling alongside as well, sufficiently close as to make the water vibrate, this is not a portion in which to linger. Here the bus had its uses after all. Shifting from bane to blessing it could be used to take our parties for a tasting in the vineyards, while someone took *Secunda* on. It was usually me who did the bus trip, leaving Philip with the barge.

Trips ashore accordingly gathered importance: to the Basilica at Vézelay, Avallon market and the Abbey of Fontenay. A burrowing into Hugh Johnson's *World Atlas of Wine*, took us further into the realisation that the liquid can be enjoyed for reasons other than getting you drunk. This led us inevitably to the region around Chablis.

The name Chablis was, at the time, confused in the American mind with any kind of dry white wine, since that was how it was sold in the States; much as the word 'Hoover' became a stand-in for vacuum cleaners. It took effort, sometimes, to point this out, with a reminder that in Europe to call a wine Chablis when it did not come from Chablis constituted an offence. And Chablis, certainly, took its wines very seriously indeed.

Wine appreciation is a dodgy subject to dwell upon, prone as it is to affectation. Circumstances count, too. Who you are with, and where, as well as what you are eating, affect the enjoyment of a wine. It took a little time to develop some confidence here, to make our way in the subject. Since, even then, Chablis wines were far from cheap, we trod cautiously for a while, asking Richard, when we met him, whom he might recommend at the outlying villages instead: St Bris, perhaps, or Irancy, characterful places where, if the wine itself was modest (it has greatly improved since) there were alternative elements to dwell upon. St-Bris in particular, was always worthwhile. The cellars there were connected by a maze of tunnels, reminders of the Hundred Years War, when armies of mercenary louts, in search of good living, headed into Burgundy and the villagers had to be organised in order to defend themselves. As with Tannay there was something about these trips beyond the stereotyped tour, with the tiniest touch of adventure to help make them tick.

To jump from here to Wythenshawe is a cultural challenge; but, back at Mission Control, Bob was striking a deal with Stanley over bookings; or an attempted one. Stanley wanted a heavy commission; but then he had the clout. We could raise our fares to cover it, maybe, so it still sounded worthwhile. With the close-the-company faction silenced for the time being at least, thanks to the gift from the *Douane*, perhaps our outfit had a future after all.

The best of the Canal de Bourgogne lies beyond Tonnerre, with only the occasional relapse - as at Montbard where, in anticipation of a popularity yet to arrive, a municipal mooring had been installed opposite the factory making steel pipes. From this the night shift could all too clearly be heard demonstrating its caber-tossing skills with the company's products.

But this is a minor quibble. You only stop at such a place once. Thereafter, the canal has a refreshing, airy quality as, the railway left behind, it rises into the sky. Heavily-locked it might be, but the keepers here, a roving squad of teenagers, would be zipping up and down on their mosquito-toned motor-bikes to wind the sluices with élan; while the glimpses of further hills, with some unpromoted *chateau* sticking above the trees, heightened the sense of adventure.

Our passengers, American, Australian and the odd unexpected Briton, fell for this area heavily. With the division between crew and paying guest increasingly blurred, another haphazardly thought-out bonfire took place.

When a member of the United States diplomatic corps steps off the gangplank into water that is surprisingly deep, the omens for the rest of the party are not good. Punch, even that made to a recipe, still needs to be contained. And the blaze was getting bigger. A retired locomotive driver from, of all places, Beverley Hills, was plainly the pyromaniac here. Most groups have one of these, sometimes several, who cannot leave a fire alone. The urge to see things burn is a basic one and the unexpected freedom we provided was too much for the vulnerable to resist.

Curbing the fire-raisers, in the condition in which they found themselves, was akin to reasoning with an obscure tribe. Shepherding them on board took a long time, with breakouts during the night. A fisherman's hut on a stream nearby had been dismembered, we discovered, then fed to the flames. It seemed wise the following morning to get away early and be gone.

Richard Parsons had his lair not far from here. High on the side of an adjacent valley, a group of farm buildings acted as a refuge. Purchased at a price that nowadays would scarcely buy a second-hand car, there was a sizable house here, together with a parcel of land and several substantial barns. In these, it turned out, lurked people on leave from the *Palinurus* and other company vessels, recovering from broken wrists, busted-up relationships, the flu and, in a couple of cases, from being fired by someone on another barge, stricter as a Captain than Richard cared to be.

Members of this community would descend from time to time to the canalside village of Marigny-le-Cahouet, which in this neck of the woods carried the redolence of Gotham City or Las Vegas, a metropolis of maybe two hundred souls. Here also at the end of the day the lock-keepers would roll in, to join the contingent in the café, for a game or two of *babyfoot*, and the usual kind of bar-room chat.

When we called by ourselves, an anti-British sub-plot was being developed. Not uncommon in rural France when the locals, digesting their pre-dinner pastis, have become sufficiently oiled to get up their bravado a little, this rarely amounts to much: a little putting-down of the *rosbifs*, as they call us, a few ribald remarks.

For Gilles, oldest of the lock-keepers, however, this was more than a principled person could take. '*Non!*' he declared, lurching to his feet as if he were Zola, putting the prejudiced in their place. 'It is not true! The English, they keep the canal open.' This was possibly so, for beyond *Palinurus* and our own good ship, few vessels came this way. Such others as there were, yachts mostly, aiming for the Med, would often be British as well. 'And what would this place be?' Gilles continued, sweeping his arm. 'Empty! Besides,' he went on, to betray the source of his loyalties, 'the English, they are kind! They give you beer!'

This could have been why, when we arrived the following afternoon at the locks he was in charge of that day, Gilles, the one with the necessary handles for winding the sluices, could only be found after a co-ordinated search with the schoolgirls on holiday who formed the rest of the *equipe*. He was behind the hedge in a field, flat on his back and fast asleep.

Into view now hove the far-from-average figure of Don. Don, after an adventurous spell owning bars in Spain, had fitted out a barge with no money, at least no money of his own. Then, as his creditors caught up with him, with the fortune that favours the brave, he attracted the interest of extremely wealthy backers. With riches in support, Don built other barges now. His stock was soaring. In immaculate white trousers, a ring on every finger, puffing on a cigar, he looked - and spoke - the part. 'Just a little project we're running up … Is that your bus? Haw-haw. We're setting up a deal with Mercedes now…'

Extravagance was Don's motto. Extravagant behaviour went with it. When he liked the brandy they served him in a bar, he bought the entire stock. Tiring of the Jaguar his benefactors provided, Don acquired a Rolls-Royce. And the barges he was putting into service, too, made Stanley's activities seem the height of parsimony.

'How did he do it?' I said to Richard Parsons once. 'Just as he was going bust, the backers of his dreams came on board his boat.'

'They are about,' Richard responded. 'But it takes a certain talent to spot them.' He looked a little rueful as he said this. Both of us had attracted backing too, but Don's was bigger. It was maddening to witness the frivolity with which he scattered around their cash.

It was Richard, ironically, who first employed Don on the *Escargot*, thereby giving him the grand idea. Then, while Richard's outfit was canvassing the high street banks, and as often as not being shown out of them again, Don was reaching for the stars. Considerations of privacy prevent a full explanation of the falling-out to come, but, before the final show-down, Don acquired not just a fleet of barges, but a farmhouse, a chateau and a replica Mississippi steamer, to be run in conjunction with a restaurant on the Yonne. Though the Rolls, in the end, would be left covered in birdshit with its tyres going flat, he had a year or two in him yet, to show how far nerve can get you.

Don's kingdom lay at the top of the Canal de Bourgogne. There, with the finance rolling in, he put together a succession of extraordinary craft, a unique mixture of clever ideas and improvisation, of brainwaves, bodging and flash. Concrete, which the rest of the boating world had learned to eschew, held no fears for Don. Into his boats it was comprehensively poured, to be followed, in at least one case, by walls built of breeze blocks. When, on an early trip, a vessel stopped suddenly in a lock, which they do if you go in crooked, some of these walls attempted to carry on, bulging and almost falling down; but Don slapped them up again, concealing their rusticity behind fabric-covered board, with a Louis XIV façade.

To Don, substance never really mattered. It was the appearance that counted. Curlicued bits of trim, bought at the do-it-yourself store in the industrial estate south of Dijon, then given a gingerbread sheen, pseudo-gold taps, marble slabs: these were the staples of his style. That his permits were obtained elsewhere on the canal system, where authority was at its most pliable, was matched somehow by the mouldings and heavy layers of paint.

It was not, at first, as if he had many clients. When, on our own trip up the Bourgogne, we sailed past his HQ, there was the workforce, out on the Flagship, painting the cabin top and polishing the portholes. 'Not busy, Don?' we enquired. 'No,' came the reply. 'Had a cancellation, dammit. Most unfortunate. But after that … phew … Don't know how we're going to cope. Got Robert Redford and Paul Newman coming the week after next...'

When we passed again two weeks later, Don's boat was still there, still being painted. With Don, fantasy and reality were intertwined. Driving around in the vintage Bugatti that was carried on the stern of one of his vessels, he was Toad of Toad Hall to the life.

Despite his outrageousness, Don would prove useful in events yet to come.

Marseilles-lès-Aubigny again beckoned now; our inevitable destination as that season drew to its end. On the Canal Latéral à la Loire, as if in preparation for England, we met the *Pisgah* again.

It was not so much the vessel that did it, English-based though she had been; it was the group on board. Coming from Birmingham, they had brought their attitudes with them.

Birmingham at the time was an amazing place, representing city reconstruction for its own sake. In homage to the motor car, carriageways and roundabouts had been created pretty well regardless of whatever had been there before. It was a building site for the sake of it. Astonishingly, in the middle of this mayhem, several of the canals in Birmingham had managed to survive. There had even been waterborne trade upon them, carried in craft that were frequently horse-drawn, their crews stomping around in a style appropriate to Chaucer.

Those on the *Pisgah* now, some of whom lived on boats there, were imbued with this spirit. The modern city they deplored; it was the alternative Birmingham that they relished, the parts connected with the waterways. Gritty and down-to-earth, the BCN as it is known - Birmingham Canal Navigations - attracted its own brand of enthusiast, folk for whom a working canal was the thing. Narrow boats in particular were what they fancied, cargo-carrying ones, not the purpose-built vessels with cabins, which were considered rather soppy.

There was a cartoon long ago in *Punch*, a painting by Rowland Emmett, in which two visitors from a spaceship were staring in amazement at a bedraggled-looking vessel on Mars. There was a Martian boatman and a Martian creature, a horse of sorts, trudging along a dilapidated Martian towpath. 'Not Barges, Charlie,' one of the visitors admonished. 'Narrow Boats!'

You have to get these things right. For this group, in particular, narrow boats were everything, or very nearly so. They had come to watch the loads going by on the Lateral Canal - steel from Rotterdam and Antwerp, some cement, but primarily the cargoes of grain, 250 tons at a go - ten times the narrow boat's average - on their way to Belgium, the Netherlands or Germany.

They were to some degree impressed; but it still wasn't the same as in England. The locks were closed at night for a start, and there were keepers, telling you what to do. They closed at lunch-time, as well! The boatmen in Birmingham would never have stood for that.

Nonetheless, the party was getting around. In Paris, on the journey out, they had even penetrated the Louvre. There, understandably, the landscapes of Breughel caught their fancy, though the Mona Lisa proved a disappointment. 'A grimy little picture,' one of them declared in his Black Country way. 'It looked like a second-hand stamp.'

Once back in Britain, they would be rejoining the working parties that helped to restore choked-up canals, getting together in the pubs each evening and sleeping in the village hall. Canals to these people, with the ethos of the narrow boat at their core, represented independence, the departure from a nanny state.

'Will you be back in England next Saturday week?' one of them enquired as we took our leave. 'We'll be going to Spindly Cripps,' he explained, naming one of the hellholes of the Birmingham system, renowned for vandalism and the rubbish beneath its bridges. 'Working party. To clear the place out. Get a great pint there at the old *Ratcatcher's Retreat*. And cheese toasties,' he added, as if that might make us want to go. We offered them a round of Bourgogne Aligoté, but they did not seem impressed.

The hunting season in France had recently begun. Men in khaki uniforms were standing on the fringes of the woods. Old chaps with shotguns tottered about, cheeks shining, to blaze away at anything that moved. Homing in on Marseilles-lès-Aubigny, we experienced the patter of buckshot on the deck. Then, following a further loud report, a mortally wounded crow fell onto the towpath out of a tree.

The hunters, we read, in their enthusiasm tended to shoot one another, with the occasional bystander along the way; but this was a good time to get our bus back to England, since the backfires it omitted were less likely to be noticed.

Heavily in decline as the season drew to a close, though still used for side-trips, the bus had been parked out of sight whenever we stopped, sparing our guests the unseemly spectacle of Penny, Philip or Mighty Min pushing it about and shouting. For the runs to Paris it seemed sensible to hire a coach, with a professional driver having the right bits of paper on him, while we nursed our own vehicle along and privately gave it V-signs. Hiccupping and banging now, down by-roads as much as we could, we made our way back to England.

There were company meetings again, first of all at Brownsworth. For old time's sake, with Portia and my brother, we briefly looked into the *Concertina*, our favoured watering hole, wondering if its capacity for incident was something that memory distorted. There was little fear of that.

Within minutes a ferocious dogfight broke out in the public bar. Two curs, each with its teeth in the other, tussled and rotated. People scattered as a table fell over. Beer went flying. Then the owner of one, seizing his pet by the tail, whirled the pair in an arc, causing further repositioning of the furniture and a massed pressing of the clientele against a wall. Advancing to the entrance he continued outside until the duo flew apart and the owner of the second one tossed his pet in the creek.

No one in the pub seemed particularly put out by this incident. Soon all were sitting again and chatting, while the hound that was banished could be seen shaking itself dry prior to fresh adventures. It was a doggie version of the bar-room scene in *Crocodile Dundee.*

Outside we bumped into Velma, the exotic neighbour from central Europe who, while *Secunda* was there, lived on the sailing barge next door. Velma worked in cabaret on ocean liners, from time to time at Brownsworth rehearsing her routines in the open air. To the bemusement of other locals, to whom a woman waving maracas was at odds with beating into the wind with the lee deck shipping it green, she would put on these displays in the car park beside the *Robber's Revenge*. Velma's husband Earl, who was a composer, mostly for TV, occasionally played piano in the other pub, developing the suspicion that she laid on these shows to taunt people.

No-one dared to challenge Velma. She was too feisty for that and, anyway, because she hated the life on their boat as much as Earl loved it, she looked down on the gumboot fraternity with a vengeance. Velma singing 'What shall we do with the drunken sailor' in a heavily sarcastic voice was a force to be reckoned with. Those of a nautical persuasion tried not to venture too close.

Reputed to sing in eight languages, she would be off soon, she reported, to perform on a cruise ship in the Caribbean. 'Something of a sensible size,' as she put it. 'But how are you doing?'

'OK. Fine, fine,' I responded, glossing over in a microsecond our financial travails, the incidents with farm animals, the dramas with buses. 'It's good …'

Saying that rather took the wind out of my sails. The list of grievances, with which I intended to unburden myself at the meeting, went unrecited. There was an odd mood when this began, in any case. Those who had cried for winding-up were sitting calmly now, making noncommittal remarks. The news that Bob, as well as garnering bookings, had been striking a deal with Stanley cast a new light over everything. Stanley wanted a heavy commission, but then he had the clout, and it still sounded worthwhile. As a further gratification most of Stanley's bookings were for whole-boat charter, for groups taking over the entire vessel for a cruise.

The euphoria developed in the weeks to come. By Christmas, Stanley's office in New York had reserved fifteen of these charter groups. Fifteen filled-up weeks! It was beyond our recent dreams. I looked into Bob's office in glowing mood. 'He loves the sea, John, doesn't he?' Mrs Gordon said afterwards.

In the euphoria generated by the Stanley bookings, two things clarified in my mind: (a) putting in more lavatories no longer mattered so much, as we were getting the customers after all and (b) there was sufficient cash coming in to support my going to Marseilles-lès-Aubigny early, to dig out some concrete. The Cortina being suspect and the bus palmed off on the Wythenshawe mafia to somehow be repaired, I went out to France on the train.

Secunda's mooring looked neater in a frost, the church spire beyond gleaming in the bright winter light. With the canal freezing over, a freight barge in passing did so with a rattling and a hammering as she forced her way along. The old chaps in the area, less inclined now to hang around by the bakery, gathered inside the village bar with the railwaymen, blurry shapes behind the steamed up-glass. At the boatyard quay those on their way to Majorca still had that voyage to come, drawing breath sharply as they chopped up wood for their stoves.

The digging of the concrete was slow. So well-mixed was it that the jack-hammer brought over by the yard's engineer, Charles, who had hired it for me in Nevers, tended to hop up and down on the surface. A day or two of this resulted in a interesting medical condition, diagnosed by those down the quay as tennis elbow, a benign-sounding term for excruciating discomfort. Put it with hod-carrier's back-pain and shot-putter's kneecap, which I also contracted, and the outcome nastier is still. The result was two days in bed.

The residue from the digging, once I could handle it again, was carted down the track for filling in the potholes. A typical Marseilles-lès-Aubigny contrivance, this was time-consuming too, but the bow was beginning to lift, so maybe the season to come would be simpler.

The Whizzer dropped by. 'On my way to Amsterdam,' he declared, while helping himself to a Cola. 'Getting a barge for myself.'

He had looked at the vessel already, and had his offer accepted. 'She's only a little one,' he continued, 'but she's fast!' There would be no *Canard*-like caution here. He had been wintering meanwhile on a friend's boat on the Nivernais, up at Clairière Endormie. There a young couple, inevitably British, were struggling to set up a boat base. 'If you think it's cold,' The Whizzer declared with relish, 'you should try it over there. Minus thirty it was. The ducks are learning to skate.'

One of the boats there, having sprung a leak, tipped on its side in the ice, to lie part submerged, at an angle. 'You know what we need?' The Whizzer had declared, after efforts to pull her upright had so far failed. 'The fire brigade! They do this kind of thing. Great big pumps! Lots of power! Good practice for them …'

A deputation went to see the fire chief, who happened to be the local butcher, and began to explain. 'A boat?' the man cried. 'Sunk in the canal?' Without further preamble he reached for a knob beside the counter, and pushed. A siren wailed. Figures tumbled into the street, buttoning up their jackets as they ran. Moments later The Whizzer and his friends were in hot pursuit as the fire engine itself, blue lights flashing, roared off up the hill.

'Be careful,' they shouted as the firemen gathered round the boat. 'There's ice on those decks …'

'These boots,' the fire chief said, tapping them proudly, 'these are firemen's boots.' As master of the situation a chuckle seemed in order. 'Whooooa' was what he said next as with a thump and a cracking noise he entered the canal.

'They lost all interest after that,' The Whizzer explained. 'Said we'd have to get the boat back ourselves. Still, it let them practice treatment for exposure. Blue as a nail he was. More haste less speed, you might say.' Which, coming from him, was slightly ironic.

With some of *Secunda*'s concrete picked out and the craters boarded over, the time now arrived to get the jack-hammer back to Nevers. This was a twenty kilometre journey each way, something I accomplished once on a bike, but without much to carry. I needed to borrow a car of some kind. Charles and John being away, the likeliest possibility was the van belonging to Herman. Herman, with his girl-friend Gerda, had arrived from Germany in this singular vehicle. They were happy to lend it too; though short of sign saying 'Find Out About Me', a more enquiry-prone machine could hardly have been invented.

In France, where police checks are a fact of life, anonymity is always the prudent course. Squads from the Gendarmerie, a pseudo-military organisation performing law-enforcement duties, hang around at intersections casing the traffic and generally being a nuisance. It pays to look ordinary.

As a challenge, Herman's van sported a mural on each side, around twice life size, in which the pair of them gazed benignly at the world in the style of royalty on a celebration stamp. If the execution was wanting, there was no lack of panache. The van, though French in manufacture, had further distinctive features. The registration plates were German, a bumper bar was missing and it listed to one side.

Amazingly, it was not until the journey back that I was apprehended. Then, sitting in the Gendarmerie's own van of the type that, because of the grills across its windows, was known as a 'salad basket', I watched the sergeant put down the details. Failure of working headlights, worn-out wipers, two bald tyres, absence of emergency triangle, lack of registration papers, absence of a spare tyre …. The list went on. Perceiving from my passport that I could not be the owner, they asked me to take this paper to whoever was and get him to explain himself. A boat hire brochure left in the chaos of the dashboard confirmed where, should he not choose to show up, the owner might be found. He was to present himself at the station at 11.30 sharp the following morning with … There followed another long list, with reference to the penalties for not having those items, and spaces for rubber stamps.

When some weeks later I asked Herman how this interview went, his reply was unhurried. 'Oh,' he said. 'I did not take any notice of it. I screwed up their liddle piece of paper and I trew it into the dock. I would not go to see them anyway,' he added as an afterthought. 'You see, I have no licence to drive.'

Had the gendarmes come to see him? No, he said. And they never did. I should have guessed. When once I was bitten by a lock-keeper's dog, reputedly unlicensed and without a rabies certificate, they never followed that up either. When I escorted an elderly and upset American into a gendarmerie down the Yonne, to report his passport being stolen, the sergeant said 'Why come and tell me?' Thus does the law fall into disrepute.

9: CHANGES OF TACK

Back injuries healed, the return to Bob's office should have been light-hearted. But no.

The news was not good. This was evident on stepping through the door. Marion, the secretary, after the briefest of greetings, was trying not to catch my eye. Bob himself was out. A pile of letters stood waiting, amongst them a telex passed on by the agency down the corridor whose machine they kindly allowed us to use. It was from Stanley, or rather from Stanley's office. Starkly, in capitals, the message jumped off the page: PLEASE CANCEL THE FOLLOWING CHARTER BOOKINGS. There were twelve of these on the list. That left three; but underneath lay another sheet. This one cancelled two more.

So, of the fifteen week-long charters upon which so much euphoria had been built, fourteen now were gone. Later I learned they had never really been 'bookings' at all, just enquiries. Once people got the details, then detected the lack of lavatories, they simply forgot about us. So, we were back to Square One - yet again. I returned to my mother's, and she made a pot of tea.

The panic those messages engendered meant a company meeting, and soon.

Staging this at a friend's house, however, was not the best of ideas. The terrible club in London would have been better. As members of the board settled into armchairs so deep it was akin to going to bed, unreality descended. It is difficult to be emphatic when your knees are in line with your nose. There were interruptions also for tea and slices of cake. As our ills were explained the atmosphere, oddly, was more of a soirée in a play by Noel Coward.

Conclusions were arrived at, nonetheless. It would be a difficult year - yet again. Bob could look for bookings. The bus might be patched up. We should try to get through, somehow. Then, the following winter, we would have those WCs installed.

Would that the job itself was so simple. Walls would need to come down, the entire cabin area rebuilt. Since parts of this were structural, these tasks could be delicate. But we must, must, must set about it as soon as we decently could - if the money could be found.

Meanwhile, we needed to employ fresh personnel. Penny, understandably, and in good time, arrived at the decision that she should develop her expertise elsewhere. Portia, too, though she could come out to help, felt the need to earn proper money in London. A new squad would have to be found.

In those days, before the Internet was invented, you placed an advertisement in *The Lady*, perhaps, maybe another in the *Telegraph*'s classified ads. The response could be large: when, as a misjudgment, we advertised in the *Telegraph* twice, we got 430 replies.

Sorting such a pile could be a hit-and-miss affair. Many admirable applicants, no doubt, fell by the wayside. The female ones, in particular, were very hard to judge, for in their entirety, almost, they ticked all the boxes. Through feminine tradition, they expected to work hard. Washing-up, tidying the cabins, making beds, attending to the laundry, serving supper: these were chores they accepted.

The men did not. They would write or phone, with the notion of it sounding good fun, meaning fun for *them*. When, at one point, while advertising for a bus driver/guide, we got a response from a man recognising that meeting new clients in Paris was bound to be a tense experience, that it was important to put people at their ease and explain sympathetically what the next few hours entailed I almost wept with joy. Unfortunately he went to work for Richard instead.

We hit lucky though; for, in the event, the crew we assembled for such a rocky, touch-and-go season backed us absolutely. Luck, the commodity specified beside the bonfire out in France, proved to be with us once again. While tributes can be boring, I must post some to our crew of that time: Dena, not only a first-rate cook, but a contributor as Penny had been; Kristin from the USA; Nicky, capable, and capable too of seeing the lighter side; and Duncan, a self-starter in a crisis.

Staying with Stanley had been a terrible waste of time. Was there anyone else who could root for us? While we had a few agents in the USA, they were scarcely balls of fire. We needed someone tougher there, to get behind us and push. And we needed deposits early, to pay for what we planned.

It was the American beside the bonfire who had suggested the game plan we should follow. The one who talked so slowly you wondered what pills he was on. It was simple enough, really.

'You need to rebuild your boat,' he had said. 'The saloon's all right. The sentiment is good. But those cabins!' New ones were definitely needed, fewer of them and larger, each with its own 'bathroom'. That was essential. 'Put it in your publicity for the year to come,' he told us, 'that you have these things. Promote it early. You'll get more enquiries. You'll get deposits. You might even get enough to pay for the conversion itself. That's what you should do in the winter.' In combination with someone in the States prepared to do that early promotion, it might still work.

Grasping at straws, I followed up a company in New England, recommended by clients that we had. We wrote to other agencies too, but attracted no great response. Optimistic Tours, however, came back favourably. They had been intrigued by barge travel, and were looking for an opening. There was hope for us in this.

Time for me, however, was running out. Thrusting the file onto Bob, I scootled off to France.

Ominously, the new season began with a series of bus collapses. Hardly had we got out to Marseilles-lès-Aubigny than it began playing up again. It was if it were a dog, brought back to somewhere it had never grown to like, going into a sulk. The clown hired in Wythenshawe, despite all his bluster, never got the engine together properly after all. How on Earth now, with this wreck, could we be expected to get through a complete season, six and a half months of it? It was the worst of starts.

Meanwhile Duncan, newly in our crew, and a real handyman, would have to keep it running. Lying underneath, he would remove the sump, let the oil drip then change the big ends. It was hardly in his job description when he signed up.

With some of the concrete removed, *Secunda* floated higher now, not by much, but sufficiently so as to let us try the southern

Nivernais again. Fumblingly, with the engine-room throbbing, we were able to make our way northwards from Decize, past the old soldier with the Salonga reminiscences, into territory that was new. That our cook might look tense here would not have occurred to me before.

In an area such as this, thinly spread, shopping was never going to be easy. There was a popular notion back home that the cook would wander round the country markets, discussing with some grinning poultryman what kind of corn his stock was fed on. It was never like that. Supplies on a much larger scale had to be found, then brought back quickly.

If in provincial France much of the old world remained, one sweeping change had certainly taken place: the erection at many a town's edge of the all-conquering supermarket. Beside the Nivernais, however, on its southern flank at least, there are hardly any towns.

Leaving the barge to press on with Duncan at the wheel, Dena and I would tear off in the bus to the nearest of these - nearest being a relative term. At the supermarket, as ever, a group would be gathered, pacing up and down, waiting for the doors to open. Such impatience is difficult to explain. With a pottering at the *boulangerie* that verges on the willful, there remains for the French, in the supermarket situation, a definite competitive edge.

At 9 am a member of the staff would drift into view, to fiddle with a key. Then, as the doors slid open, with jaws assertively set, an army of revved-up shoppers went streaming through the gap - until, around twenty yards inside, the music overtook them. As if struck by a sedative spray, they stumbled to a crawl.

Whoever chooses the tapes for supermarkets might rule the world. Riots could be controlled by them. Spectators at football would be suspending their hostilities to give one another flowers. It takes willpower to ignore this influence, those anaesthetising strains. Panic helps too. Could we select a thousand pounds-worth of food and drink in time to get it past the tills, reach the canal again, find the boat, yet still do lunch? Tempting though it might have been to examine the two-for-one deal on baking trays , it was vital to put the blinkers on and keep going.

With fourteen passengers and a crew of five, sometimes six, the food and drink required amounted to a bachelor's shopping list multiplied many times. As the numbers increased on board, too, so did the amount of wine consumed per person. There are few better places to buy middle-of-the-road wine than one of these places, incidentally, for the powerful organisations behind them strike calculated deals.

An impressive number of trolleys would be filled on these visits, each parked while we went off to fill another, in the hope that some member of staff would not assume the contents to be there for re-stocking, then stack them back on the shelves. This did happen once, and sorely disruptive it was.

It was vital now to put the goods through the checkout in order: food first, since it was at 5.5% Tax Value Added, then drinks at 17.6%. Following that came household items, also at 17.6%, but, by taxman's decree, to be listed separately, if we wished to reclaim it. After the till, at the manager's office another bill had to be made out, addressed then certified with the company stamp.

In finding *Secunda* again the canal map would be helpful now. At a cruising speed of four kilometres an hour on this waterway (six on any other) and a quarter of an hour for each lock, a calculation could be made. At the canalside, the state of the water might tell us more. A light brown colour meant a little boat had passed, dark brown a bigger one, almost certainly ours, as she was deeper and stirred up more mud. Cross-hatched patterns on the water indicated passage within the last ten minutes. The trick now was to get to a bridge or lockside to meet *Secunda* as she arrived, so that the goods could be heaved on board without the hassle of the gangplank.

In later years - if there were to be any - we might organise a regular supplier, and place the orders in bulk, safe in the knowledge of the numbers on board, and sticking to a regular route. But we were some way yet from being settled enough for that.

Whack, bongle, bang. These were not good noises to hear. We had knocked a blade off the propeller. Without passengers, thankfully, having just waved them farewell, we were moving *Secunda* along a tad, when it happened. 'Some big stones under that bridge,' a lock-keeper stated, rather too late. While the boat continued to move forward, she did so slowly now, hopping up and down as she went.

As bad news goes, this, in the arcane world of barge operation, is serious stuff. On the Nivernais, on the western Canal de Bourgogne and the Latéral à la Loire, it is mega-serious. There are no effective dry-docks.

In the whole of this region, despite the increasingly specific regulation of vessels, with the need for detailed surveys , there is not a single such dock of consequence (well, at Marseilles-lès-Aubigny on a good day, if the vessel is shallow enough, or Migennes on the Canal de Bourgogne, where it is shallower still).

Not far south of Baye, however, stands a set of staircase locks. Here, going briefly into anorak detail, one lock chamber directly empties into another. There are complicated reasons why this, in the long term, is not a good idea. Staircase locks waste water, and favour the traffic continuing in the same direction, rather than alternating, as elsewhere. For the sorely pressed, however, the arrangement offers one advantage: that a chamber can be drained, to make a primitive kind of dock. In this, with a bit of trouble, we might get at the propeller.

Barge propellers, made out of iron, are generally hefty. A fully-trained weightlifter might have snatched up our spare one to goolie height before running out of steam. Getting this on and, equally seriously, getting the old one off, like many things to do with canals, promised an exercise of the kind that got Stonehenge erected, or built the very first tanks.

Being near the locks was one stroke of luck, being without passengers another. But our main good fortune lay in attracting the attention of Monsieur Cretier, who ran a trip boat down towards Nevers, who knew about barges, having been born on one, and who was married to a keeper nearby. He is dead now, alas, but he deserves his place in Heaven.

Not only was his advice invaluable, he had a propeller extractor with him, for getting the old one off, to be clamped over the wreckage like a metallic kind of squid. Then you whacked it with a hammer. Of benefit also, Monsieur Cretier went along beforehand to the Canal HQ in Corbigny and asked them what the heck they were playing at in denying us permission to use the so-and-so lock. Did they not realise, etc? Under his onslaught, thankfully, 'No' became 'Maybe', then 'OK', but at our 'own risk or peril', a common enough get-out in France. Whoever might or might not carry the can was the last thing on our minds.

So, on what should have been the 'evening off', with a friend, Edward Bonel - one of the few who escaped the Superglue possessiveness of Marseilles-lès-Aubigny, and who lived on a boat nearby - we changed the prop.

Though the level could be dropped, there was still a fair bit of water around, so we worked from the dinghy. Whirling a metre-long mooring spike mallet is by no means easy from a dinghy, since the latter moves as well. It puts a new perspective on osteopathy. So did winching up the old prop and lowering down the new. But in the end it was managed. The whole job took many hours, and without Monsieur Cretier's help we could be in there yet.

Having been thwarted in our earlier attempts, reaching Baye from the south represented something of a triumph. There, we could treat our new guests to the view across the lake that we cherished.

After this, continuing northward, we would be in familiar territory again: the tunnels and the cuttings, the dramatic flight of locks, then onwards towards Auxerre. It was a surprise, on passing, to find Pierre no longer there. His cottage, now empty, looked across forlornly as we worked our way through. 'Have you not heard?' asked the woman keeper there. 'He went into hospital. Not for the first time,' she added with a gesture to indicate that drinking on such a scale had taken its inevitable toll. 'And he died there last month.'

So, no more presentations of the paper now. There would be no clarification either; certainly not here. His wife had moved away. The woman now working the lock had little else to say.

It was not much farther down the canal to Tannay where, the following day, we visited the winemakers again. Unexpectedly now Madame Moreau was able to throw further light. 'Yes,' she said,

'He was one of ours. He used to be chauffeur at the chateau. And in the *Maquis*, too. I'm not sure if that letter he showed you was actually meant for him ...' She gave a shrug. 'But no matter.'

Why, we wondered, had she declined to mention this earlier? There came a partial explanation. 'There are many around here who do not care to be reminded. It is not lightly talked about. Usually, when you come to see us here, you have others with you. Unless I know who I am with, I get in the habit of changing the subject.'

Pierre, it transpired, was at the Battle of Crux-la-Ville, which none of us had heard of, despite it being one of the most important confrontations in the history of the French Resistance. It involved a force of 4,500 German troops, heavily armed, with artillery in support, in addition to aircraft used for bombing and strafing the *Maquis* positions. Their objective: to deal with the Resistants once and for all. In so doing they would be clearing a path for the massed reinforcements that their army wished to move from their south-western garrisons to the new theatre of warfare in the north. They were thwarted by an assemblage of largely amateur soldiers, many of whom had never fired a weapon before. This was desperate fighting, the *Maquis* group Mariaux, hugely outnumbered, holding out for four days before breaking free. With other Resistance groups arriving, the Germans then had to withdraw.

And where was Crux-la-Ville? Why, across the lake from Baye, beyond the trees on the farther side. The *Maquisards* of the area impeded German forces at a vital time. No wonder the Americans had been grateful.

Yet folk said 'Nothing happened.' How could they?

'Well,' said Madame Moreau, 'your country was never occupied was it? Now,' she concluded, 'let us try the Sauvignon. Hmm, a little young, perhaps, but it promises well....'

Shortly after we arrived in Clamecy, The Whizzer got there too. Roaring in with his new barge, he rushed alongside, lassoed one of our bollards, then hopped on board.

His boat was called the *Bourdon*, which is French for bumblebee. Bumbling though was not in The Whizzer's nature. With the vessel already part-converted by some previous owner in the Netherlands, it would not be taking him long to finish the job himself. Meanwhile, he proposed to have a good time.

As full of tales as ever, he had generated more on his voyage. Coming out of the river Oise, he discovered the Seine in flood. 'Roaring, it was' he said with glee. 'Absolutely roaring.' Struggling to the outskirts of Paris, the *Bourdon* took refuge behind the island at Issy-les-Moulineaux until the flow died down.

Borne on the current, various things came floating by: crates and planks, masses of branches and, eventually, a corpse. A passer-by saw it, caught in a tree across the water. The passer-by found a policeman, who found other policemen who, because they needed his dinghy, called out The Whizzer. 'I didn't want to look at it,' he said unconvincingly. 'It's arms were all floppy. Ouaggh.' He gave a mock shudder.

'Was it a man or a woman?' asked Nicky.

'Neither!' said The Whizzer in triumph, having tempted his audience into a suitable state of curiosity.

There was a moment's pause before the punchline. 'Know what it was?' he asked. 'An inflatable doll from the sex shop. Amazingly realistic, though. You should have seen the gendarmes' faces. Now then,' he added, as practical requirements took over. 'You couldn't let me have a pack of Pepsi, could you? I'm completely out of it.'

With phone-boxes around at last, it was possible to liaise with Bob on the project with Optimistic Tours, and to learn of a meeting.

Their people were coming over from the States and staying a day or so in London, Bob reported, before resuming some other mission that they had, apparently with yachts in Greece. It would have been better, obviously, if they could have come to France and actually seen *Secunda*. But at least they still seemed keen. And so, in a week without passengers, I went over to London to meet them. So important was this that I caught the plane and flew.

It was a bright sunny day in Park Lane, where, just a few yards from where our company began, we entered another hotel. There in the lounge waited Sal and Bud, effusive representatives of Opimistic Tours.

We had white wine spritzers, a novelty then (and a definite non-starter in the vicinity of Chablis, but we did not dwell on this). Our contacts were enthusiastic. One or other of them would like to visit *Secunda* shortly, sure thing. Yes, they reckoned, they could start marketing, soon. Well, within a month or so. Their commission was reasonable, the promise to send deposits as reassuring as it was vital.

This, on reflection, was a far better arrangement than we might have entered into with Stanley. What had seemed a disappointment could now be regarded as a narrow escape.

As we parted in Park Lane, shaking hands and smiling still, the sun came out again and Hyde Park glowed. In the resulting euphoria we could revise our forecasts. With the money these people looked like bringing in, we might even spend a bit now.

Just a month or so later, the clouds lifted farther still, Hector was in touch, and the news was staggering. Beyond the wildest dreams of our start, we would have a new bus. The old one, not even worth the ferry fare back to England, could perhaps be left at Marseilles-lès-Aubigny for someone with time and determination to restore. Or maybe keep their hens in.

Better still, the new bus would be French. No longer would muttering mechanics be confronted with the need for bits and pieces, as they saw it, from a troublesome land. No longer would there be the need to hire two other, smaller, vehicles in the vicinity of Auxerre - for had the old machine been spotted there, the sky would have descended.

With the new bus, there were further regulations. It would have to be inspected, often. Yet in France, notwithstanding, a British bus-driver's licence would do. We learned this from Richard's business partner Guy, a founder member of the mutual aid society that, with a few abstentions, supported anyone trying their luck with a barge.

Back in Cheshire I had managed to pass a driving test for machines of this size, in a vehicle borrowed from someone in the trade. I was proud of this, for bus-driving tests had differences from the norm. First of all, the examiner tried to wind you up. 'Of course I saw that road-sign, you stupid old fool' was what they were aiming to hear. Then they failed you. Getting through this, despite the provocation of the stupid old fool sitting beside me at the time, was hopefully a measure of my increased tolerance on the rocky road to success.

With the bus itself came a forest of paperwork, put together by the long-suffering secretary of the character with a hairline moustache and flow of corny patter with whom, on the outskirts of Paris, we finally struck the deal. *'Oh, les femmes!'* he would say putting his arm around his colleague's' shoulders and winking. 'Sign here,' she said to me resignedly, 'And here.' Our bank account would be depleted each month as the stage payments were drawn. The interest rate was considerable, but it was the only way we could do it.

Soon enough the *Douane* showed up again. For this was the year in which, alerted by the rumours of further vessels plying, they decided to sort this out. Import Duty: have you paid it? That was the battle-cry.

In *Secunda*'s case, of course, this had already been done, but it did not prevent them enquiring again one morning at Clamecy. There an elaborate ambush had been set - for ourselves only, for there were no other craft about. Officers in full uniform assembled, escorted by a squad from the local police.

Entering the lock to greet this crowd, our passengers must have wondered if they had been granted some kind of civic reception. It took a little time to recognise the leading figure. With a stripe down his trousers, heavy epaulettes and a kepi, he was certainly dressed to impress. 'Oh,' he said as our eyes met and the realisation dawned. 'We've met before, haven't we?' It was the foxy character, the one outside the bakery. And there, amongst the other ranks, was his heavyweight chum, squirming a little at the occasion. They were pouncing on a vessel they had visited already.

Heaven knows what cock-ups like this must cost. An elaborate raid had been launched on a vessel investigated the year before. There wasn't even a bus to delight in. For form's sake I invited a few of them on board, to mingle uncertainly with folk from Boston, Massachusetts, while they made a show of going through our papers. But, basically, it was time badly spent. As they got up to leave, the leader, the one from the bakery, asked if we had any foreign stamps. 'I collect them,' he said. A rummage by our passengers yielded some American ones, with a couple more from New Zealand. So his morning, at least, was not entirely wasted.

'Dear John,' the letter began, and the rest can be deduced. We should never have trusted Optimistic Tours. None other than Eric James had moved in, approaching Optimistic just as our own deal was about to be sealed. The *Campagnarde de Bourgogne*, big and ostentatious, appealed to them more - and Eric wanted exclusivity, to be the only one. There was lots of mealy-mouthed stuff in their letter; but, basically, we had been dropped.

To say that the air was blue was to understate the situation. It was positively indigo. Eric! He had stolen our lifeline from us! Where was the bugger?

A spot of local enquiry tracked Eric down. He was at Lagny on the Marne, or would be later in the day. So said the lady in one of Auxerre's hotels, which Eric used as a gathering point and centre for his mail. 'Shall I tell him who called?' She was smiling as she spoke, as if Eric was the acme of charm.

Lagny, on the eastern fringe of Paris, was a two and a half hour drive away. But it was our own day off, so called, without passengers and thankfully without any belts to tighten. I would go over and see him and ... What? It was fortunate really that it was such a lengthy drive, for it gave a little time to think. Perhaps, face-to-face, it would be possible to talk him out of it?

Getting to the quayside at Lagny first, I stood there looking serious as Eric's great ship arrived. He scarcely looked pleased to see me, but could hardly not invite me on board. There were passengers gliding around, from one handsome lounge to another, then to a bar, where Eric had a guy with a black bow tie serving complicated cocktails. In a private area near the stern the pair of us shuffled from one foot to the other as I asked him to reconsider and he thought of reasons why he couldn't.

'You see, John, we will be paying for advertising - a considerable amount' As he did not look me in the eye right then, I somehow questioned his version of 'considerable.' As a diversion, and possibly to get me onto the shore again, he took me on deck to demonstrate the new version of a gangplank he was developing. Gangplanks, always awkward, can be tiresome indeed. Eric's was clever: a long wide walkway, stored on its side against the rails when the vessel was moving, then swung out when needed, with support from a wire up above. Fundamental to this process was an elaborate joint.

Eric swung it out, tipped the plank to lie flat, then adjusted the support. At which, with his sleeve snagging on the wire, the plank moved a little and the joint, seizing its opportunity, jumped from its housing and tumbled into the Marne.

'Oh, dear,' I was just able to say. 'How very disappointing.' It was fortunate, perhaps, that a couple of Brazilian ladies - it was typical of Eric, somehow, to have latched onto Brazil as a source of clients - came out and asked him where the shops were.

It was plainer than ever now that he wanted to be rid of me; but, endeavouring to be suave still, he made a concession.

'Before I met the Optimistic people,' he declared, 'I did consider a couple of other companies.' And he gave me their addresses.

I rang Bob that evening and once the expressions of rage were over, he said he would give those two a try.

Secunda was moored at Cravant when all this happened, a small town where the Route Nationale crosses the Nivernais canal. Returning to the basin there, I found the on-board tanks almost empty. Already in no happy state of mind, I had to pursue the need for drinking water.

For some reason the people I spoke to thereabouts always had a lisp. A thin, elderly man coming out from one of the houses asked me what I wanted. '*De l'eau*,' I responded and he waved at the canal. 'No, no, drinking water. I need a tap, *un robinet!*' My accent may not have been the best, but it was generally understood.

'Un lobinet?'

'Oui, oui, un robinet'

'Quoi?'

'Un robinet.'

'Un lobinet?'

This could have gone on some time. In the end I drew him a picture of what we needed. Suddenly, the penny dropped.

'Ah,' he exclaimed, comprehension spreading across his face. '*Un lobinet*'

'Yes, yes …'

'Oh, you won't find one today,' he declared, his manner now kindly. 'You see, it's Sunday.'

'So ….?'

'Yes. The shops are all closed. You'll never buy one now.'

We were swimming against the tide again, I decided. Even finding a water tap had become a problem. The news at the end of the week, though, was better.

'Spoke to those two companies,' Bob said. 'The Washington one was hopeless,' he went on, my heart sinking yet again. 'The guy there didn't have a clue. Thought you could get from Paris to Nice and back in a week. Told him they didn't have canals at Nice. Sounded surprised. But the other lot, McGuinness, they sounded good. Woman there called Jill. She thinks there's something in it. Wants to come on board … I'll see what I can do.'

So, there was hope again - yet again, yet again, yet again ….

10: SURVIVAL

It is strangely true that, at a mooring, someone coming to see you drives a vehicle differently to those visiting for other reasons, to fish perhaps, or simply take a look. There is something about the crunch of the gravel, the closeness of the parking, to signify a person with a mission. From down in the engine-room, where I often was, such arrivals always generated a frisson.

The approach of a car travelling faster than any, followed by a skidding noise and the cry of '*Merde*' as bumper met bollard on the quay signified the more eccentric kind of visitor. This would be The Whizzer, who had bought himself a saloon of the old-fashioned kind, with windscreen wipers like toothbrushes and enormous headlights. He had also acquired a hound, a floppy-eared mongrel, intensely loyal already, with that beguiling canine grin. Being rescued from the dog's home, she was delighted now to be riding shotgun beside The Whizzer, gazing through the windscreen as if the outfit were all her own.

What The Whizzer's clients would make of this ensemble had yet to be revealed; for, like others before him, he was discovering that passengers are not so easily enticed. He had, nonetheless, managed to take a group of friends, prepared to put up with the rusticity of a boat that was, after all, only recently bought. Otherwise, with admirable spirit, he had been running forty-minute trips at a town up the valley, during a fête beside the canal.

There, from a platform beside the waterway, with a background of announcements and the blaring of the band, were these voyages on the *Bourdon*. Paid for by the Chamber of Commerce, it was a fifteen-minute voyage each way between the quay there and a turning point down the line. The *Bourdon*, her decks crowded, had been busy throughout the weekend.

It was towards the end of this affair, The Whizzer said, that while manoeuvring at the downstream end the vessel got heavily stuck. Vessels often get stuck on the Nivernais. It is no big deal, but the to-ing and fro-ing to get free does stir up the mud. As an angler shouted to us once on *Secunda*, 'There's so much muck here now I'd be better off fishing in the garden!' A similar thing had happened with the *Bourdon*.

Anglers by canals can sometimes be a pain. There might well be other places to sit, other watercourses with no boats whatsoever, but the knack such people have of choosing spots where navigational procedures are guaranteed to take place verges on the uncanny. After crouching there for hours, occasionally mauling the fish but otherwise sinking into gloom, they can develop a tendency, too, by no means universal but common enough, to look for scapegoats. When a particular vessel that has been bothersome all day comes along yet again to turn the canal into heavy-duty soup the temptation becomes irresistible.

The angler The Whizzer fell foul of had a building by the waterside, a kind of summer-house, in which to retreat and muse, gazing from time to time at the rods on stands, with a line of floats beyond. Seeing the *Bourdon* arrive for the umpteenth time, then get stuck, the owner, dancing out and shouting, let fly with a handful of gravel.

No-one was damaged, though one or two cried out, and a woman sitting on the cabin top was struck, not too violently, but struck all the same, by a bouncing bit of stone. At this her husband, in Hawaiian shirt, droopy shorts and wide straw hat advanced upon The Whizzer to explain that, though he might not look it, he was in fact head of the Gendarmerie.

'Have you got a gun?' he enquired, for all the world as if it was a handkerchief he was asking about. 'Well,' said The Whizzer, not sure where this might lead, 'Yes, I have, actually.' It was an airgun of some kind, powerful enough to slay the rats plaguing a quayside when coming down from Amsterdam. 'See the windows in that man's hut?' the man enquired. 'Ye … s' came the response. 'Well, you shoot them out.'

'I can't do that,' The Whizzer protested.

'Yes you can,' said the Police Chief. 'An eye for an eye and a tooth for a tooth.'

So The Whizzer did. There were lots of windows, but he was a good enough shot and those on board were supportive. By the time of his next trip downstream, two officers with the salad-basket van had got there as well, noting name and address and generally being officious about it all

'Something else that Police Chief said,' The Whizzer now went on. 'Is that the *Douane* will be around again soon.'

'Well, they've been to see us already,' I was able to say.

'New subject,' The Whizzer advised. Whatever now?

'Red fuel,' The Whizzer announced.

The panto that followed when the *Douane* next descended, was worthy of an operetta. Red-stained diesel oil, marked in that way to denote a lesser rate of tax, was available for domestic heating. For years, also, it had been used in boats. Then the law was changed and the privilege withdrawn. That might have been the end of it - had not the people in Paris who ran the *bateaux-mouches* kicked up an almighty fuss.

These large glass-enshrouded craft, of which there are many, contribute substantially to the tourist income of the city. They carry a lot of clout. So the edict on fuel came to be suspended, while some kind of fudge was dreamt up. The revised judgement, when it came, was remarkable. Red fuel, it was announced, could still be used in some vessels, if not with others. Those getting away with it - guess what? - included passenger-carrying craft running to a published timetable.

The Whizzer, who happened to be carrying a further group of pals when this decree was enforced, met the requirement by producing a timetable of his own. 'Depart Grande Place, Monday: 0900 hrs,' he wrote. 'Arrive Petiteville (Café Des Sports): 11.30.' And so on, all the way through the week, until a final arrival at Le Port - in practice a raggedy-edged old basin with metre-high blades of grass - at Chitry-les-Mines at 19.15 hrs on the Friday. But, according to the *Douane*, this did not count.

This ludicrous business went on for an age, with the supplementary excitement of the authorities using a helicopter. This came into play because Jaap, who had turned up recently from the Netherlands, realised very quickly that the customs people only came to places where there was a major road alongside. Adjusting his activities accordingly he took to terminating his voyages, which were only for four people anyway, and on a bed-and-breakfast basis at that, to a loop of the Yonne south of Auxerre and amongst the woods of Nièvre. The *Douane* never got to him.

It is over-dramatising to describe this issue as a 'battle'. Quarrel might be the better term, a long-drawn, tedious wrangle, short on humour or understanding, dragging on, as these matters seemed to do. But into it plunged the charismatic figure of Don.

Don had recently brought to Auxerre his latest vessel, a stunning mixture of exotic veneers and heavily painted fibreboard. Too big to get up the Nivernais, she was not the kind of ship anyone might ignore. The cabins were big - massive by comparison with ours - the saloon so twinkling with chandeliers it might have been a shop set up to sell them. There were lavatories also: en suite WCs, of the household type their users could understand. That was the brilliant part. Not so good was the tank into which they emptied, neither big enough nor in the right place on board.

Under the impact of a newly-arrived party of guests, the tank, on the very first evening at Auxerre, soon became full. Don, in the middle of his opening speech on deck, having been told of this situation in a whispered aside, broke off for a moment to instruct his crew to pump it out. 'But ...' the messenger ventured. 'Pump it out,' Don declared, 'Into the river! Now!'

It was the wrong place to do this, at the wrong time. He had not got the outlet right either. It was far too high. With an enthusiastic roar, the pump played its part. A sheet of nasty-looking stuff sprayed across the Yonne, as the group on deck, travel agents from the States, invited on board to be impressed, retreated as if swept by a brush.

Detail was never Don's game, but he had the bluster to carry things off. The *Douane*, in picking on him, were unfortunate to have done so. With few bookings to speak of, yet masses of money, he could do battle with these characters and give them a bit of their own back.

In the days of the fuel enquiry - which turned into months - Don held centre stage. Whosoever he met got to hear all about it: of the lawyers he was hiring, the latest stand in court. To have actually gone to court was breath-taking. Don was fighting these battles up-front, 'on behalf of the industry,' as he put it. It was highly impressive: no-one had ever referred to us as an industry before.

What Don had was nerve, colossal nerve. When hot-air ballooning reared its complicated head, Don laid on one of the biggest gatherings ever, beside the railway line from Paris. There, by arrangement, a luxury train was stopped so that the occupants, after drinkies on Don's barges, could take to the air in style. As a promotional effort it was a fantastic achievement, mind-boggling in its complexity. It was a pity, on the day, that it was windy.

The fliers, well-heeled people from the higher echelons of gossip-column society, having been serenaded and had their pictures taken, now found themselves whirled across the countryside at considerable speed. With the pursuing fleet of vehicles whizzing up farm tracks and around the backs of sheds, and Don shouting his instructions as if he were General Patton, it took time to recover them all. Landing a balloon in these conditions is by no means easy. At lower speeds than this, reputable ballooning companies take care not to set out. Folk get dragged through hedges or into ditches. It can be nasty.

At the time of Don's great venture there were still no mobile phones, so the scattering was more prolonged. Those on board became lost, to be retrieved hours later, weeping and with their clothes torn. Recrimination ensued, but Don, being Don, said how fantastic it all was, and poured out masses of Krug.

Don gave to our activities something of a Malibu flavour. Gentle exploration, the stroll through the long grass: those things were not for him. But he drew the fire of the *Douane*. And when, after going to court the last time, to the highest court possible, since he had lost in all the others, he finally won, it would have been churlish not to be grateful.

Years later I was told this victory was due to the *Douane*'s advocate getting the date wrong and not turning up. Like other Donnish stories it is hard to disentangle his own version from the real thing, but he did us all a favour, for the use of red fuel continued as before.

Don has gone from the waterways now, variously reported to be in Goa, imprisøned in Mexico, or married to an heiress there. The truth remains elusive. Our thanks must be recorded, nonetheless.

Jill, the lady from the McGuinness company, came on board one week, and said that she liked it. Or she liked what the boat could become. There at short notice, with a mixed group of people, she fitted in well. So another deal was constructed. They would promote, we would rebuild. They really seemed to mean it.

We had another excellent cook in our later stages: Rosemary, not only great in the galley, but a moving spirit of cheerfulness when all otherwise might be sliding into a shambles.

We survived that season on the bookings Bob could send along. An embargo on maintenance helped also, made possible to a considerable extent by our having a decent bus. The monthly payments we now were making looked to be less than we spent at garages with the vehicle we had with us before.

The tally of equipment failures on *Secunda* was shorter now, but, as that season drew to a close, we had a vintage one. The innovatory German heater, situated as so many things had been, at a point where only the double-jointed might reach it, gave in at last and blew up. Located under the upholstery at the side of the saloon, it had never run satisfactorily since the days of our launching party at Brownsworth. There Bob, while hosing down the boat, and in the course of impressing a lady called Mary Rogers, sent a quantity of water into the outlet grill and drenched the electronics. Luke spent the rest of that evening taking the circuitry to pieces and grumbling, but it never ran properly after that. Switching itself off at times unconnected to requirement, it began to glow threateningly whenever it was on.

When it exploded, which it did in a cold snap at Bailly, pieces of metal pinged about briefly beneath the cushions. Meanwhile through the air vent came a lump the size of a cricket ball, revealing itself to be smoke of an unusually condensed kind. This quickly expanded, to fill the saloon with the smell of Guy Fawkes Night, while our guests at the table, wide-eyed for a moment, faded behind a cloud.

We bought a portable heater for those last few weeks, something else we might have provided at the start, had we not been so experimental.

As to the intended conversion, where should we be doing it? The thought of Marseilles-lès-Aubigny just engendered gloom. It was a long way off for starters. There would be the diversions it always threw up. There were the freight trains.

No, we decided: Auxerre was the place. At Auxerre, instead of a cement factory in the background, there was an abbey and a cathedral, in fact one of the finest waterfronts in the world. There were suppliers near at hand, shops, all manner of eateries, even a cinema should the work get on top of us. It was cheering to think of: Auxerre The Golden. So that was where we went.

Waiting on the quayside as we arrived was The Whizzer. Hopping excitedly at the thought of the extra suppers we might provide, he happily took our ropes. As usual, he was full of gossip and intrigue. Not only did he have the details of the lock-keeper's wife-swapping saga at Cuisses-des-Cultivateurs, but also he knew where to get fuses and belt drives. He could also deliver a round-up on our competitors, on the fiasco of so-and-so the cook walking out in the middle of an entrée, on other people's disasters with their plumbing. Which made us think we had not been so bad after all.

As we packed up for England, I found myself explaining to The Whizzer the alterations we would be making. 'This wall will be going. These two cabins will become one, with the shower over here.' And so on. As I described it all, the effort it would involve - and the expense - became more apparent. With precious little in the bank right now, we would be relying on deposits from McGuinness. If these did not come in, if this deal fell through, then (how many times had this been said before?) we had had it. Should we do it, or should we not?

'It's not going to be easy, knocking down these walls,' I ventured.

'You reckon so,' said The Whizzer. 'Why don't we see?'

'Er, hang on a minute …' But we had drunk several Kirs.

'Well, come on. You said you were going to do it. Why not now?'

Once in the swing of it, it was fun. In a hail of plywood and tiles The Whizzer became visible through a partition as he battered

Luke's painstakingly erected showers into a myriad of tiny pieces. It was a scene from *The Shining*. Electric wires began to emerge, an indication of detailed work to come. There was dust. Once this had settled there came the realisation: going back could be difficult now. Conversion or bust!

It was irresistible, whilst back in Britain, to tour old haunts. At Brownsworth, in the tradition of that place, feuds were still raging. Someone in the nautical trade was renting his property from someone else; although the latter, it emerged, did not actually own it. At the moorings, Velma, returning from her Caribbean excursion, had managed to slip off the gangplank as she arrived, making an impression as of a skydiver holding out a suitcase when she landed in the mud.

An ultimatum to Earl apparently followed that. There could be no more of this living on a vessel that cost a fortune to keep afloat; that because of the tides was not even in water half the time, but sat in chocolate-coloured custard; that had to be approached up a plank and was the object of ridiculous attention from a gang of guys with beards whose womenfolk, when there were any, would never have graced the Folies-Bergère.

Barges were not for Velma. It had been brave of her to give them a try. So Earl was seeking out a house for them to move to. There was the matter of the parking tickets as well. These Earl collected by the bagful because, on his trips to the recording studios in London, in the beat-up car that he ran, he never had the time to find a proper place to leave it. His theory, that it was only the last of these offences that mattered, since all previous ones got cancelled under the weight of municipal book-keeping, was being disproved by some very expensive letters.

'Sick of this country, John,' he declared, while unburdening himself in the *Concertina and Spittoon*. 'There's no scope for initiative here ...' His income from composing jingles for television advertising had come under scrutiny also. 'Who are these co-composers, with whom you are so generously splitting your royalties?' the tax office enquired. To which the response of 'Oh, some people I was sitting with in a café in Madrid' was being treated with doubt. 'You know, John,' Earl declared. 'I envy you what you are doing. At least you don't get people coming after you over tax, things like that.'

'But we do, Earl, sometimes,' I had to tell him. 'We do.'

At the Wythenshawe office the usual mini-dramas were being played out. In the room next door Bob was on the phone. 'Look, Alan,' I could hear him saying, 'This is serious. One of your drivers has been involved in an accident. It's no good just saying it wasn't his fault. We need the details. What? Hang on, I can't hear you properly ...... Mrs Gordon!' He was starting to shout. 'Could you put the phone down please?' There was a rattling noise as Mrs Gordon, who was holding the extension earpiece to rub it with a duster, dropped it, said 'Oh, dear' into it when she picked it up, then clunked it back on its mount. She wandered off humming, to lift the cover off a typewriter in order to spray its innards with cleaning fluid.

'Where was I?' I could hear Bob enquiring.

'Have you ever been to Australia?' Mrs Gordon said to me then. 'They've got those life-saver people there.'

There was news, occasionally, from the McGuinness camp, and even bookings. Well, not quite bookings yet, as we had not had any money from them. Mindful of the Stanley debacle, we trod cautiously now. The conversion could be planned, but not acted upon as yet. I scarcely dared tell the others of the walls already knocked down.

Christmas passed, then, one day, a letter arrived. Inside was a substantial American cheque. We were saved! But were we? Dollar cheques took an age to clear, six weeks on average in Britain. Yet we no longer had six weeks left. They ought to have sent a Direct Bank Transfer as we asked. Should we contact McGuinness now, and say we would tear up the cheque, if only they would do this instead?

Let's not rock the boat, we decided. Those earlier let-downs made us hyper-cautious. So, instead, Bob set up lunch with the bank manager who, by the time the pudding was served, and undoubtedly on the strength of Bob's own business with him, said he could lend us the dosh meanwhile. There would be things to sign of course. This left things tight; but, I reckoned, we could just fit in the conversion before the first of our customers turned up.

We had been drawing up lists of materials to buy in England: plywood, since the stuff in France was appalling; paint, hopeless there, had already been compared to brushing the walls with milk. Portia, taking time off from her proper job, could help me load the stuff into our bus, then come with me to Auxerre.

There were drawbacks to this process. British materials might be better. They might also have been half the price. But they had to be 'declared'. Customs officers lay in wait at Calais or

Dieppe and, unless you had Form T2, the discussions could be tiresome.

You got this form filled in at Dover. There, in cabins beneath the cliffs, freight agents, the counterparts in England of the *transporteurs*, tackled the paperwork in exchange for their challenging fees. Nor did the expense stop there, for, once the form was completed, the ferry company charged extra for what had suddenly become a 'commercial load'. It was a great temptation to smuggle.

Amongst the lessons learned was never to write 'Calais' as the intended destination. There long-distance lorries, supposedly a rapid means of transport, sat sometimes for days as the *douaniers* picked their way through the list. The queues could be immense, particularly over a weekend when the customs shed closed down and a mass of drivers wandered into town to drink cheap beer and play on the pinball machines.

Far better was Auxerre, where the customs depot could be found in the industrial estate. It was prudent also to write 'pine' for any description of timber, since other materials were enquiry-prone. And to inscribe '24 volt' regarding any electrics, since they might otherwise be rejected for not being on some French-recognised list. No-one from the *Douane*, in our experience, ever came out to verify these items. Nor did the *transporteurs*, who sat in the very same compound. They just kept you waiting, and it was sensible to take a paperback when you went.

When, after years in the 'Common Market', France, Britain and the other countries finally united in a free trade area, these practices came to an end. Down at Dover, freight agents, their workload slashed, staged a demonstration. But their heyday seemed to be over.

Burgundy during winter can be cold. No longer in the countryside are there sunflowers, or villagers standing in the shade. During summer, it is hard to accept that a time will arrive when a boat's engine must be drained, her water pipes disconnected. Yet, with a wind sweeping over from Poland, even Auxerre can succumb. To arrive in February, as Portia and I did, when the Yonne was thinking of freezing and a regular noise each morning was the sound of cars colliding, made the thought of settling down to work a serious challenge.

Job Number One, while trying not to shake from the cold, was to get the stove going. Job Two, which became apparent as the ship filled with smoke, was to install a new chimney. The old one had corroded through.

There was a store up in town that might sell such things. Sure enough, in the basement there were racks of them, arranged according to size. Seeing me measuring these, the man in a smock who was serving called across.

'What is it you want?'

'A stovepipe chimney'

'What size?'

'Sixteen centimetres diameter.'

'How long?'

'Two metres.'

'We haven't got one.'

'Yes, you have. They're in a third of a metre lengths, and you've got six of them.'

'You can have two.'

Those in the queue turned like a row of dolls to gaze.

'Why only two?'

'Because if I sold you all six, there wouldn't be any left for anyone else.'

Portia intervened. 'If we come three times and buy two each time would that be alright?'

There was a muttered reply to this, at which we took what we needed, slapped down the requisite number of francs and departed.

'Don't you ever come here again,' the man shouted.

With heat on board at last, the water system, disconnected at various points, could be put together, and the ship's plastic hose brought in to thaw. Then more hose, until there was sufficient to reach a tap down the quay that, being inside a building, had not been turned off in the frost. With that achieved it became possible to have a wash. Getting to that point took the better part of a day.

Our carpenters were due to join us that evening, a husband-and-wife team, encountered the previous autumn when one of Don's smaller craft managed to clobber the local bridge. Harry and Paula had come out to put things right. English yet again, Harry and Paula were carving out a new career, fixing things on barges. They had worked on *Escargot* too, in a similar scenario to our own - installing en-suite WCs.

Seizing the opportunity, I'd had a word, offered a wage, then signed the pair up. Fortunately, because there were other jobs they could work on, in people's houses, they were flexible as to timing. There were conditions all the same: at least one day off a week, however panicky we became. A pal had a cottage beside the Canal de Bourgogne, they said. Each Saturday evening, they would be retreating to that.

Before the *Escargot* job came up Harry and Paula had been running a pub in London. Running a pub, as it turned out, was what they really wanted, in the countryside for choice. Running one off the Edgware Road in London, which is what they had actually been doing, with the Anglo-Polish-Irish clientele given to fearful acts of violence, did not entirely fit the bill. Which was why they were carpenters again.

Another condition was that, in addition to meals during the week, a reasonable amount of beer should be provided, since, given their background, they had developed a liking for it. So, while shopping in Leclerc, I swept up a package of the stuff. There were twenty-four bottles of light Alsatian lager - not, probably, what they preferred, but enough to set them on the road, so to speak, while tastes were identified.

It was a couple of hours before supper when they arrived; but in less time than that all twenty-four bottles had gone. They were nice about our running out, and were happy to make up the difference in wine, but plainly, from then on, beer-buying would be a serious priority.

To their credit, this nightly bacchanalia did not slow them down. Their jaws did drop when they realised there were fourteen new doors to hang, but they handled that bane of the house-fitter's life with commendable determination. The money spent on beer certainly seemed to be working.

More bookings were coming in now, even deposits, and by Direct Bank Transfer too. Unexpectedly almost, McGuinness were actually living up to their promises. Hector, who, from the Cumbrian hills, was master-minding the currency transfers, felt we might soon be paying our way.

We also had a chequebook in France, a major breakthrough, hampered only by the post office in Auxerre refusing to hand it over. It was addressed to our company, not to me. The company articles were requested, a laborious portfolio put together at last by the Chamber of Commerce in Bourges. From the post office I walked back down to the boat to get this. Then I returned.

There was still no joy. 'I see your company is registered in Cher, Monsieur. This is the département of Yonne.' What we still had to do, apparently was go to the Chamber of Commerce and get our registry transferred. Only then would she hand the chequebook over. Resisting, with difficulty, the temptation to leap across the counter and grab it, I felt it easier afterwards to write to the bank asking it to send all correspondence to my mother's place in England. Here the postman, without hesitation, would hand over a letter to the Nazi Party if it was Hitler who came to the door. It was no surprise to learn, a little later on, of Tony Paris's problems when the post office he went to farther south had filed all his mail under E for Esquire.

With three weeks left before the season began, there were four weeks of work still to do. Someone, somewhere, may have done such a job in comfort; but, these many years on, I have yet to hear of it. It was vital, all the same, to take a break occasionally. 'The brain gives out before the body does,' Luke used to say, and if we slogged on through the weekend, as some of us did, it all became half-paced.

Despite the growing hysteria, Harry and Paula, sensibly, continued to have their Sundays off. Each Saturday evening they would take themselves away to the lock-house of their friend at Marigny-le-Cahouet, there to gaze at the stars and no doubt consume the odd few drums of ale.

As to the rest of us, on Saturday evening, after supper, at some risk of falling asleep in the stalls, we would visit the cinema. Ah, Marseilles-lès-Aubigny: if only they'd had a cinema there! What would they have shown one wondered? Documentaries on cement production, probably. And the film would have broken half-way through. There was something uplifting about Auxerre, a great place to emerge after a late-night showing. We seemed to be making some better moves at last.

Completing our work was touch and go, of course. It had to be. It is a barge-fitting tradition. Putting in those lavatories was complicated. The way the *Secunda* had been assembled back at Brownsworth, with essential props amongst the walls, meant the cabins could only lie a certain way. From the fourteen passengers we previously might take, we were down now to a maximum of ten. But we could charge better money and the formula, very soon, would at last be paying its way.

On the final night before the customers arrived, we had, as I had always promised, a glass of the local sparkling Crémant each. Then I made an awkward speech. Then we went back to work again.

‘Welcome on board, ladies and gentlemen,’ I was able to say the following afternoon, standing though I was in front of paint not entirely dry.

We were at last in the state we should have been in when we first started out.

POSTSCRIPT

In compiling this account, one or two names have been changed. But, broadly, it happened as described.

Barge cruising continues today in France, and there are more craft now. The *Secunda*, modified at last, ran with increasing success - so much so that we eventually bought another barge; none other than Richard's *Palinurus*, which we tore apart and completely rebuilt - with en-suite WCs, of course - under the name of *Luciole*. This time we had a better idea of what to do. *Secunda*, ultimately, was sold into private hands, a hotel-barge no longer.

Our own mistakes in barge design, laughably obvious now, were a little less so at the time. We were unlucky perhaps in starting when we did, when the conventions of boating were different. Had we come in even a single year later, our path would have been clearer. And if romance and irrational decisions overcame common sense, one only has to look at the boardroom workings of Association Football - or banking - to see that it still goes on.

Stanley and his wife in the end pulled out of their own operation, detaching themselves absolutely. Others then ran it. It is important to stress this in view of the subsequent difficulties of the company and its eventual collapse. Busy their barges may have been, but they were too expensive to build - the downfall of many who take to the water. Boats do not just cost more than outsiders believe. They cost many times that.

The *Janine* survives under another name, having been possessed by the *Douane*, then left in a sunken condition on the Canal de la Marne au Rhin. Richard's company rescued her and licked her back into shape.

Eric James, having found Optimistic Tours a non-starter after all, sold his vessel at a judicious moment, then left France behind him. Our own agency contact in the States, however, worked very well for us.

Regarding the Resistance movement in France, the battle of Crux-la-Ville, unjustly overlooked in the memorabilia, was described in detail by a local businessman, Hubert Cloix, when sufficient time had passed for a calmer view to be taken. It is an heroic tale, in which Hubert Cloix himself, then a student, played a significant part. There is a sense in his account of bewilderment at the lack of recognition - to some extent rectified by the more recently established Resistance Museum at St-Brisson and by the erection of plaques where actions took place in the area.

While there are now several books in France concerning this period, it is difficult to escape the feeling that their publication comes only as the generations directly involved gradually fade away. John Lichfield, writer on France in *The Independent* newspaper, considered in 2008 the reaction to an exhibition of photos taken during the Occupation - photos showing, by and large, the citizens of Paris going about in a manner not that different from today. He quotes an elderly Resistance leader from the Auvergne: 'We knew the people who were on our side, or we thought we did. We also knew who the active collaborators were … The people who scared us were the rest… At any given moment you could never be certain which side they were on.'

Hence the guardedness we encountered. France's difficulty 'to look its wartime self in the face,' according to John Lichfield, can be blamed upon Charles De Gaulle, who created in 1945 'the myth of a martyrised, unbending France, betrayed by a minority of traitors. The truth, as he knew better than anyone, was much more opaque and much more human.'

For books in English on the Resistance, *SAS: With The Maquis* by Ian Wellsted covers, from a soldier's point of view, the activities in the Morvan, and at one point near the Nivernais Canal. *Maquis*, by George Millar, is a definitive account, set farther east, near Besançon.

The waterways of France are popular today. No longer is the Canal du Nivernais run in the Clochemerle fashion that we encountered, although there still can be problems, of detachment by those in charge. Enthusiasm is a vital commodity in running a waterway.

Following the disappearance of tariff barriers at last, the *Douane* rarely appears now, but there are many more rules for boat operators; technical ones mostly - with precious little information for the unwary, or discussion in any public forum. With the absence of regulations in Britain when we first went over, and the relaxation of certain French ones when at last it became apparent that the hire-boat industry was an economy-booster, it is difficult to avoid the impression that in France the imposition of laws is more a matter of habit than any desire to ease the way.

As to ourselves, our company revived in many respects. At the height of our problems one or two directors resigned, but that was all. Conviviality returned when fortunes got better. Bob, able at last to leave passenger-gathering to others, moved in time to a more salubrious neighbourhood - losing contact with Mrs Gordon, although she made her reappearance one day in a suitably bizarre situation ....

The traffic was bad that morning, very bad indeed. The cause: one of those abnormal loads that creep along by lorry at a barge's pace, the kind that in other countries do in fact go by water. At Wythenshawe itself, at the critical roundabout, an overhead cable got in the way and the vehicle had to stop.

The police were there on their radios, the haulage crew standing around while someone somewhere, Heaven knew who, could be contacted about cutting off the power. Then …

'Oi! Use this!' It was Mrs Gordon, advancing down her garden path with a clothes pole. It was a wooden pole, with a notch on the end, and with it one of the team could stand on the truck and lift the cable clear.

The problem solved, Mrs Gordon took her pole back and the commerce of Manchester resumed its giddy ways.

We shall miss her. And the many other good souls who came and went on our adventure. Adventure: you don't have to climb Mount Everest to experience one of those.

THOSE INVOLVED

Our crews: Penny T, Portia, Mighty Min, Philip, Pippa, Dena, Duncan, Rosemary - and many more. Bless them all.

The Measurement Man - may his socks have holes in them.

My fellow directors - in particular Bob, Hector, John S, Betty, my brother Peter, Peter Feversham and Luke - without whom the idea would have faded away and I would have been left holding just a few bits of paper, and a boat no-one else would have wanted.

Richard Parsons, who passed on the grand idea.

The late Tony Paris, much missed now. He never let the rules get him down.

Chris and Vanessa, of *Pisgah*. With hospitality at judicious moments, and with their bus, they provided support when needed.

The Whizzer, who kept liveliness in it, still.

Archy, the provider of sanctuary, and help, at *Waterways World*.

John Riddel, the man who invited us to Marseilles-lès-Aubigny, the best of moves, since it gave us time to sort things out.

My mother, who kept me going, and kept me together, when the outlook was bleak.

Monsieur Bertrand, who, behind the official exterior, was kind.

Customs men: at Calais, Bourges, Auxerre, and points in between, upholders of regulations even they found difficult to understand.

The late Peter Zivy, who, before anyone else realized its potential, kept the Canal du Nivernais in being by launching a business there.

Madame Moreau, Pierre, Uncle Henri, Monsieur Cretier, Gilles and all the lock-keepers and maintenance men who accepted our intrusion and, in many cases, helped.

Jimmy and Clara, explorers with the *Canard*.

Manny, the weaver of many a dark brochure. And Tony, our designer, who could bring it back to life again.

Rene Guichard, driver of an obedient pair of mules, at a time all others had forgotten how to do it.

Don, larger than life, who bested Authority in the end.

Herman and Gerda, providers of a peculiar vehicle (They have become more respectable since).

Eric James, supplier of the agency address that got us going - in the end.

Sal and Bud, Jarrett and Stanley : potential sellers of our cruises.

Jill, who did sell them.

Earl and Velma, who kept Brownsworth in order.

Harry S, originator of a freezer that, even today, would baffle the combined forces of Heath Robinson and NASA.

Harry and Paula, who rebuilt the boat, cheerfully, and with great competence.

Mrs Gordon.

Our passengers, who often found a vessel that was wanting. Yet again, and again, and again, they made the best of it, and gave incalculable support by so doing.

With my deepest gratitude. JL. May 2009

JOHN LILEY

As a small boy in south Lancashire John Liley played beside, and in, the derelict Ashton Canal. When, in 1952, his father organised the first of many trips on the English waterways, he discovered 'an alternative world, a throwback that seemed likely to end at any moment.'

Years of sailing followed. He has crossed the Atlantic on a schooner and helped to deliver yachts between points as far apart as the Shetland Isles, the Canaries and the eastern shores of Greece.

On joining *Motor Boat & Yachting* magazine in 1963 he was amazed to find the canals of England still surviving - 'if only just, and they were constantly under threat. The waterways of England had to be campaigned for, against all the forces of a blinkered regime.' John took the magazine into that fight and, on becoming Editor, found himself arguing the case for, amongst others, the Ashton Canal. It is now open to navigation again.

Leaving the magazine in 1972, he explored the waterways of France, then Germany, the Netherlands and Belgium in 'a beat-up old English coal barge'. A spell with *Practical Boat Owner* followed, before he pursued a career with the hotel-barge *Secunda*, described in these pages.

Marriage and the birth of three sons have limited these activities, but, from a home base in Cheshire, he still visits France often. Amongst other books he has written are *Journeys of the Swan*, covering adventures on the English canals, *France - the Quiet Way* - a guide, and *Barge Country*, an exploration of the Netherlands.